A TEST O

THE WESLEYAN CENTENNIAL EDITION
OF THE COMPLETE CRITICAL WRITINGS OF LOUIS ZUKOFSKY

Volume I

A Test of Poetry

A
TEST OF
POETRY

LOUIS
ZUKOFSKY

FOREWORD BY ROBERT CREELEY

"Trust to good verses, then"
—Robert Herrick

WESLEYAN UNIVERSITY PRESS
PUBLISHED BY UNIVERSITY PRESS OF NEW ENGLAND
HANOVER AND LONDON

Wesleyan University Press
Published by University Press of New England, Hanover, NH 03755
© 1948 by Louis Zukofsky
This edition copyright © 2000 by Paul Zukofsky, Sole Heir to and Executor of the
Estate of Louis Zukofsky and Celia Thaew Zukofsky
Foreword to the 2000 edition © Wesleyan University Press
First published in 1948 by the Objectivist Press
First published in England in 1952 by Routledge & Kegan Paul Ltd.
Republished in 1964 by Jonathan Williams, Jargon Books, Highland, North Car-
olina, in association with Corinth Books, Inc., New York, N.Y.

Printed in the United States of America   5 4 3 2 1

CIP data appear at the end of the book

ACKNOWLEDGMENTS

for lines from *XLI Poems* and *Ampersand* by E. E. Cummings, copyright, 1925, by E. E. Cummings.

for lines from *Is 5* by E. E. Cummings, copyright, 1926, by Horace Liveright.

for lines from *Leaves of Grass* by Walt Whitman, copyright, 1924, by Doubleday Company,
Inc.

for lines from *The Waste Land* by T. S. Eliot, copyright by Harcourt, Brace & Company, Inc.

for translations of Catullus by F. W. Cornish from The Loeb Classical Library edition, copyright by Harvard University Press.

for lines from "Death" in *Collected Poems* by Mark Van Doren, by permission of the publish-
ers, Henry Holt and Company, Inc.; copyright, 1939, by Mark Van Doren.

for lines from "Alisoun" in Jessie L. Weston's *Chief Middle English Poets*, copyright by
Houghton Mifflin Company.

for "Another Weeping Woman" reprinted from *Harmonium* by Wallace Stevens, by permission of Alfred A. Knopf, Inc., copyright, 1923, 1931, by Alfred A. Knopf, Inc.

for lines from William Morris' translation of Homer's *Odyssey*, copyright by Longmans,
Green & Company, Inc.

for lines from "Timing Her" in Thomas Hardy's *Collected Poems*, copyright, 1925, by The
Macmillan Company and used with their permission.

for lines from "Blood and the Moon II" in William Butler Yeats' *The Winding Stair*, copyright, 1933, by The Macmillan Company and used with their permission.

for "Moonrise" from *Poems of Gerard Manley Hopkins*, used by permission of Oxford University Press and the poet's family.

to Marianne Moore for "Poetry" and to Basil Bunting, Lorine Niedecker, Charles Reznikoff
and William Carlos Williams for the use of their poems.

CONTENTS

FOREWORD

There's little a fledgling poet can look to for advice as to how best to "test" his or her own work, given the mass of apparent poetry now so simply available. Years ago I felt it a blessing that poems, given books and libraries, could always be got to despite whatever difficulties. They seemed so enduring, a dependably common fact, in all their various record and publication. One knew that there were the great works prior to literacy. These must be the foundation of any poetry at all, one thought, even though so much had been lost in the shifts of time. The very way of thinking a world, and of finding order within it, all had changed forever with the advent of reading and writing. Perhaps that was a loss one could not in any way calculate. It must certainly have been a very different practice, pruning as it went, revising as it found itself echoing the same words, the same stories, collective, spoken, never far from an actual music. Learning slowly myself, I wondered if that way would have been a less lonely undertaking, more communal, shared, as it seems still to have been at times for friends who were musicians, when they played a common song. Louis Zukofsky spoke of his poetics as "upper limit music, lower limit speech," echoing these same concerns.

But a poetry certainly survived, still hearing, sounding, ordering in a way specific to its earlier nature, despite it was no longer decisively the culture's means for securing the "tales of the tribe," the society's locating information of habits and history. But what in this changed world would be its practical economy? What were the locating definitions of its art? How might one presume a measure, a way of knowing that *this* was the effective means, that *that* was not? It could hardly be that a proposal rested simply upon one's taste. Ezra Pound had dealt with that presumption effectively: "Damn your taste! I want if possible to sharpen your perceptions after which your taste can take care of itself." Zukofsky's own proposition has a simple elegance:

> How much what is sounded by words has to do with what is seen by them, and how much what is at once sounded and seen by them crosscuts an interplay among themselves—will naturally sustain the scientific definition of poetry we are looking for. To endure it would be compelled to integrate these functions: time, and what is seen in time (as held by a song), and an action whose words are actors or, if you will, mimes composing steps as of a dance that at proper instants calls in the vocal cords to transform it into plain speech.

> —"Poetry," in *"A" 1–12* (Origin Press edition, 1959)

Sight, sound and sense, and how each has to do with the other, and how words themselves form a company—all gave me an immediate locus, a place where I might put my own experience in reading, hearing, seeing, whatever it proved words were saying, or doing.

No doubt Americans particularly love systems, demonstrable procedures, a "how to" for whatever engages them. *A Test of Poetry* is certainly a great work of this kind. But it has also another characteristically American quality, a feeling of inevitable singleness. By that I don't mean "singular," not "lonely"—but *alone.* "Alone" as Emily Dickinson was alone, as Whitman was, despite the friends and neighbors, as W. C. Williams puts it: "I was born to be lonely, / I am best so!" One recognizes the exceptional attention Zukofsky has given to the work of assembling these materials. This book is no anthology or any such generalizing collection of texts. It is a continual process of selection, of weighing alternatives, and becomes a *common book* of self-determined and tested examples—what has stayed by Zukofsky, what he knows well.

Rightly or wrongly, poetry demands such a concentration—just as the weighing, feeling, thinking and choosing of all these instances here offered must insist. If, as Williams wrote, "To measure is all we know . . . ," then the accuracy and evident perception in that "measure" becomes a critical factor. So, again, these examples are hardly a random sampling—or what Zukofsky might have found simply as the usual cultural baggage of the time. Rather his work here is to make a concentrated attempt to be specific, to define, to locate the sufficient evidence, to make a full register, to practice a responsibility, to discern crucial differences, to "Trust to good verses, then . . ."

I cannot now remember how long it took me to move out into the open water of Parts I and III of the "Comparisons." My earlier advice had been Ezra Pound's *ABC of Reading* and so I spent days pondering the information Zukofsky compactly gives in Part II. In some respects the commentary of the middle section makes a "walker" for the novice, positing standards, demonstrating values, making explicit judgments. When finally I ventured into Parts I and III, I still secured myself by flipping back to the index repeatedly, to see who had written what. It was as if I had to keep checking the label so as to be convinced of the goods. How many hours has one wandered in museums, with all their glorious prospect, squinting to read tags and identifications, so as to be reassured one's response was appropriate!

Pound was intent on telling the reader what he, Pound, thought the reader should know, providing little room for other reflection. Reading, one simply followed the brilliant leader. But Zukofsky's work was differently addressed, even though he stated his observations just as firmly. "What is foreign to poetry is the word which means little or nothing—either as sound, image, or relation of ideas. If, in any line of poetry, one word can be replaced by another and it 'makes no difference,' that line is bad." It remains a practical advice. Toward the end of "Wales Visitation" Allen Ginsberg interjects suddenly, "What did I notice? Particulars!" Then follow the closing lines, having to do with a literal physical place and feeling. Elsewhere Ginsberg tells the story of going to Williams, asking to be told about prosody, and of Williams sending him on to Zukofsky as the one who might help him.

In that way this is an intimate book, both for its author and for its readers. I think a great question always for either is the nature and fact of the relation presumed to exist between them, what after all they think to share. "Poetry is that art for which no academy exists," Robert Graves had written, but I understood that comment to mean that there was nowhere one might go to school to learn the requisite procedures, no elders available as fostering teachers, no determining or apparent standards. Insofar as poets were at best often marginal in the society, frequently masked by other occupations or professions—Zukofsky taught compositional English at Brooklyn Polytechnic Institute for a good part of his life—poetry's art was necessarily a compact of lore, of precedent learned from its masters, rules of thumb handed on in like manner—genius, chance, good luck, and an abiding trust of the kind Robert Herrick makes so clear.

Poets of my company loved Zukofsky. Paul Blackburn, Cid Corman, Gilbert Sorrentino and Robert Duncan—all felt him an absolute master. Duncan, I remember, first gave me *Anew* to read (together with Williams' review of it) in 1954 just after Edward Dahlberg, visiting in Mallorca where I then lived, had asked me why we young poets did not work to secure Zukofsky and bring him actively into print. So it is that Zukofsky's contributions to the *Black Mountain Review* became a constant, and the first substantial printing of any part of his major poem, *"A"*, is accomplished by Cid Corman's Origin Press in Japan. *(A Test of Poetry* itself is brought back into print by Jonathan Williams' Jargon Press in 1964, following his initial publication of *Some Time* in 1956.) Much as one might go to college, we put ourselves to school with Zukofsky. His skills, we felt, were the greatest of our time.

All that seems another edge of history now. But as you read and think of what is to be found here, how it calls to mind insistently a various meaning, how it feels its way, how this manner of saying something may be more direct, perhaps, than that, remember—*Oh fathers and teachers!*— that this is the same way Zukofsky went, and that this is what he found.

ROBERT CREELEY
Buffalo, N.Y.
February 18, 1999

PREFACE

The test of poetry is the range of pleasure it affords as sight, sound, and intellection. This is its purpose as art. But readers have rarely been presented with comparative standards to quicken their judgments: "comparative" in the sense that the matter with which poems deal may be compared. To suggest standards is the purpose of this book. By presenting for comparison several translations of the same passage from Homer, an elegy of Ovid and lines from Herrick that read like an adaptation of Ovid, or a fifteenth century poem about a cock and a recent poem about white chickens, and so on, a means for judging the values of poetic writing is established by the examples themselves.

If the poems of Parts I and III, which have been presented anonymously, interest the reader he should be moved to decide for himself their relative merits, without reference to their authorship.

In Part II the poetry has been accredited for the convenience of historical explanation. I have summed up the criticism of this part in a footnote of very few words, in the chronological chart. As I say there, the criticism probes only my own considerations. I believe that desirable teaching assumes intelligence that is free to be attracted from any consideration of every day living to always another phase of existence. Poetry, as other object matter, is after all for interested people.

Louis Zukofsky

PART I

COMPARISONS

" . . . the comparison I am drawing is far too rigorous to allow me to use these statements without being fully assured of their accuracy; yet I have no right to supress them, because, if accurate, they establish what I am labouring to put on an undoubted foundation. . . . "

MICHAEL FARADAY

1a_____*

Arrived now at our ship, we launched, and set
Our mast up, put forth sail, and in did get
Our late-got cattle. Up our sails, we went,
My wayward fellows mourning now th' event,
A good companion yet, a foreright wind
Circe (the excellent utterer of her mind)
Supplied our murmuring consorts with, that was
Both speed and guide to our adventurous pass.
All day our sails stood to the winds, and made
Our voyage prosperous. Sun then set, and shade
All ways obscuring, on the bounds we fell
Of deep oceanus, where people dwell
Whom a perpetual cloud obscures outright,
To whom the cheerful sun lends never light;
Nor when he mounts the star-sustaining heaven,
Nor when he stoops to earth, and sets up Even,
But night holds fix'd wings, feather'd all with banes
Above those most unblest Cimmerians.

1b_____

When we were come unto the sea-side, where
    Our ship lay, which we shov'd into the deep;
We rear our mast, pull up our sails, and bear
    Aboard with us one male, one female sheep.
And so for Hell we stood, with fears in mind,
    And tears in eye. But the fair Circe sent,
To bear us company, a good fore-wind
    That kept our sails full all the way we went.
To winds and steerage we our way commend,
    And careless sit from morning till 'twas dark;
Then found ourselves at th' Ocean's farthest end,
    Where up to land the wind had forc'd our bark.

*This space may be used by the reader who enjoys marking up his copy
for evaluating the compared examples of similar object matter under
each cardinal number in some such way as *great, good, fair, poor.*

1c_____

For hell we launched with two sheep to sacrifice
And trimmed the gear despite our tears.
But Circe saw to it the wind came aft
Until the sails were filled with it all day.
We sat, steered, nothing to do.
Then the dark: a deep river — alien
To our world — where the Cimmerii live:
In cloud and fog no sun ever
Broke, or a star. Beached in pitch-dark;
Then with the sheep in our arms, followed
The shore to wet hell
As Circe had promised.

2a

And paid our respects in hell: Perimedes and Eurylochus
Held the sheep, while with my sword I dug the pit,
About a forearm in length and about as wide,
Pouring into it for all the dead, forgetting none,
One after the other, mead, fragrant wine, water, sprinkling of
    barley-meal —
Praying over and over to each unbodied head
Vowing that at home in Ithaca
I would sacrifice the priceless cow
And pile treasures on her fire,
And to Teiresias besides offer the prize black ram.
On this word, I cut the sheep's throats,
Their blood splashed the pit,
And then the dead flowed — crowds from below,
Brides, virgin boys, old men tried in hardship,
Little girls hurt,
Slain soldiers, the wounded armed —
All clamoring —
My blood paled.

2b

Thus solemn rites and holy vows we paid
To all the phantom-nations of the dead,
Then dy'd the sheep; a purple torrent flow'd,
And all the caverns smok'd with streaming blood.
When, lo! appear'd along the dusky coasts
Thin, airy shoals of visionary ghosts;
Fair pensive youths, and soft enamour'd maids;
And wither'd elders, pale and wrinkled shades;
Ghastly with wounds the form of warriors slain
Stalk'd with majestic port, a martial train:
These, and a thousand more swarm'd o'er the ground
And all the dire assembly shriek'd around
Astonished at the sight, aghast I stood,
And a cold fear ran shivering through my blood;

2c———

The blood flowed dark, and thronging round me came
Souls of the dead from Erebus — young wives
And maids unwedded, men worn out with years
And toil, and virgins of a tender age
In their new grief, and many a warrior slain
In battle, mangled by the spear, and clad
In bloody armor, who about the trench
Flitted on every side, now here, now there,
With gibbering cries, and I grew pale with fear.

3a_____

The Golden age was first; when man, yet new,
No rule but uncorrupted reason knew;
And, with a native bent, did good pursue.
Unforced by punishment, unawed by fear
His words were simple, and his soul sincere.
Needless was written law, where none opprest;
The law of man was written in his breast.
No suppliant crowds before the judge appeared;
No court erected yet, nor cause was heard;
But all was safe, for conscience was their guard.
The mountain trees in distant prospect please,
Ere yet the pine descended to the seas;
Ere sails were spread, new oceans to explore;
And happy mortals, unconcerned for more,
Confind their wishes to their native shore.
No walls were yet, nor fence, nor moat, nor mound:
Nor drum was heard, nor trumpet's angry sound;
Nor swords were forged; but, void of care and crime,
The soft creation slept away their time . . .

To this next came in course the Brazen Age:
A warlike offspring prompt to bloody rage,
Not impious yet . . .

Hard Steel succeeded then;
And stubborn as the metal were the men . . .
Then landmarks limited to each his right;
For all before was common as the light . . .
And double death did wretched man invade
By steel assaulted, and by gold betrayed.

3b_____

Then sprang up first the golden age, which of itselfe maintainde
The truth and right of everything unforst and unconstrainde.
There was no feare of punishment, there was no threatning lawe
In brazen tables nayled up, to keepe the folke in awe.

7

There was no man would crouch or creepe to Judge with cap
    in hand,
They lived safe without a Judge in every Realme and lande.
The loftie Pynetree was not hewen from mountaines where
    it stood,
In seeking straunge and forren landes to rove upon the flood.
Men knew none other countries yet, than were themselves did
    keepe:
There was no towne enclosed yet, with walles and ditches deepe.
No horne nor trumpet was in use, no sword nor helmet worne.
The world was such, that soldiers helpe might easly be for-
    borne . . .
    Next after this succeeded straight, the third and brazen age.
    More hard of nature, somewhat bent to cruell warres and rage,
But yet not wholly past all grace. Of yron is the last
In no part good and tractable as former ages past.
    . . . and men began to bound,
With dowles and diches drawen in length the free and fertile
    ground,
Which was as common as the ayre and light of Sunne before . . .
The spurres and stirrers unto vice, and foes to doing weel.
Then hurtfull yron came abrode, then came forth yellow golde
More hurtfull than the yron farre then came forth battle bolde
That feights with both, and shakes his sword in cruel bloudy hand.

4a_____

The flouds at random where they list through all the fields did
    stray,
Men, beasts, trees, corne, and with their Gods, were Churches
    washt away.
If any house were built so strong, against their force to stonde,
Yet did the water hide the top: and turrets in that ponde
Were over whelmde: no difference was between the sea and
    ground,
For all was sea: there was no shore nor landing to be found.
Some climbed up to the tops of hils, and some rowde to and fro
In Botes, where they not long before to plough and Cart did go,
One over corne and tops of townes whom waves did over whelme
Doth saile in ship, an other sittes a fishing in an Elme.
In meddowes greene were Anchors cast (so fortune did provide)
And crooked ships did shadow vynes, the which the floud did
    hide.

4b_____

It is but even a little droppe that keepes us two asunder.
He would be had. For looke how oft I kisse the water under,
So ofte againe with upwarde mouth he ryseth towarde mee,
A man would thinke to touch at least I should yet able bee . . .
Thou dost pretende some kind of hope of friendship by the
    cheere.
For when I stretch mine arms to thee, thou stretchest thine like-
    wise,
And if I smile thou smilest too: and when that from mine eyes
The teares doe drop, I well perceyve the water stands in thine.

5a_____

Mentula has something like thirty acres of grazing
land, forty of plough-land: the rest is salt water.
How can he fail to surpass Croesus in wealth,
who occupies so many good things in one estate,
pasture, arable, vast woods and cattle-ranges and lakes
as far as the Hyperboreans and the Great Sea?
All this is wonderful: but he himself is the greatest wonder of
    all,
not a man like the rest of us, but a monstrous menacing Mentula.

5b_____

Tradition said he feather'd his nest
Through an Agricultural Interest
    In the Golden Age of Farming;
When Golden eggs were laid by the geese
And Colchian sheep wore a golden fleece
And golden pippins — the sterling kind
Of Hesperus — now so hard to find —
    Made Horticulture quite charming.

A Lord of Land, on his own estate,
He lived at a very lively rate.
    But his income would bear carousing;
Such acres he had of pasture and heath,
With herbage so rich from the ore beneath,
The very ewes' and lambkins' teeth
    Were turned into gold by browsing.

He had rolled in money like pigs in mud,
Till it seem'd to have enter'd his blood
    By some occult projection:
And his cheeks, instead of a healthy hue,
As yellow as any guinea grew
Making the common phrase seem true
    About a rich complexion.

6a⎯⎯⎯

Thay umbeset the seyis bustuously
Quhill fra the depe till euyrye coist fast by
The huge wallis weltres apon hie
Rowit at anis with stormes and wyndis thre
Eurus, Nothus, and the wynd Aphricus
(Quhilk Eist, South and West wyndis hate with us.)
Sone eftir this of men the clamour rais
The takillis graffillis cabillis can frate and frais.
With the cloudis, heuynnys son and daiyis lycht
Hid and brest out of the Troianis sycht
Derknes as nycht beset the see about,
The firmament gan rumyllyng rare and rout
The skyis oft lychtned with fyry leuyn
And schortlie baith are, sea and heuyn
And euerythyng manissis the men to de
Schewand the ded present before there E.

6b⎯⎯⎯

I boarded the king's ship; now on the beak,
Now in the waist, the deck, in every cabin,
I flamed amazement: sometime I'ld divide,
And burn in many places; on the topmast,
The yards and bowsprit, would I flame distinctly,
Then meet and join.   Jove's lightnings, the precursors
O' the dreadful thunder-claps, more momentary
And sight-outrunning were not: the fire and cracks
Of sulphurous roaring the most mighty Neptune
Seem to besiege, and make his bold waves tremble
Yea, his dread trident shake . . .
                    Not a soul
But felt a fever of the mad, and play'd
Some tricks of desperation.   All but mariners
Plunged in the foaming brine, and quit the vessel,
Then all afire with me: the king's son Ferdinand
With hair up-staring — then like reeds, not hair —
Was the first man that leap'd; cried, "Hell is empty,
And all the devils are here."

7a_____

Round, round, the roof does run;
 And, being ravished thus,
Come, I will drink a tun
 To my Propertius.

Now, to Tibullus next,
 This flood I drink to thee.
But stay! I see a text
 That this presents to me:

Behold! Tibullus lies
 Here burnt, whose small return
Of ashes scarce suffice
 To fill a little urn.

Trust to good verses, then;
 They only will aspire
When pyramids, as men
 Are lost i' th' funereal fire.

And when all bodies meet,
 In Lethe to be drowned,
Then only numbers sweet
 With endless life are crowned.

7b_____

Therefore when Flint and Iron wear away,
Verse is immortal, and shall nere decay.
To verse let Kings give place, and Kingly shows,
And banks ore which gold-bearing *Tagus* flows.
Let base conceipted wits admire vilde things,
Fair *Phoebus* lead me to the Muses springs.
About my head be quivering myrtle wound,
And in sad lovers heads let me be found.
The living, not the dead can envy bite,
For after death all men receive their right.
Then though death rakes my bones in funeral fire
I'll live, and as he pulls me down mount higher.

8a_____

This ae nighte, this ae nighte
    Every nighte and alle
Fire and sleet and candle-lighte
    And Christe receive thy saule.

If ever thou gavest hosen and shoon
    Every nighte and alle
Sit thee down and put them on
    And Christe receive thy saule.

If hosen and shoon thou ne'er gav'st nane
    Every nighte and alle
The whinnes sall prick thee to the bare bane
    And Christe receive thy saule.

8b_____

I sing of a maiden
    That is makèles;
King of all kinges
    To her sone sche ches.
He cam also stille
    There his moder was,
As dew in Aprille
    That falleth on the grass.
He cam also stille
    To his moderes bour
As dew in Aprille
    That falleth on the flour.
He cam also stille
    There his moder lay,
As dew in Aprille
    That falleth on the spray.
Moder and maiden
    Was never none but sche;
Well may swich a lady
    Godes moder be.

8c———

Erthe out of erthe is wondirly wroghte,
Erthe has geten one erthe a dignite of noghte
Erthe appon erthe hase sett alle his thoghte,
How that erthe appon erthe may be heghe broghte.

Erthe appon erthe wolde be a kinge;
But how erthe to erthe sall, thinkes he nothinge.
When erthe bredes erthe, and his rentes home bringe,
Thane schalle erthe of erthe hafe full harde partinge.

Erthe appon erthe winnes castells and tourres,
Thane saise erthe unto erthe 'This is alle ourres';
When erthe appon erthe hase biggd up his bourres,
Thane shalle erthe for erthe suffere scharpe scourres.

Erthe gos appon erthe as golde appon golde.
He that gose appon erthe gleterande as golde,
Like as erthe never more go to erthe scholde,
And yit schall erthe unto erthe ga rathere than he wolde.

Now why that erthe luffes erthe, wondere me thinke,
Or why that erthe for erthe scholde other swete or swinke
For when that erthe appon erthe is broghte within brinke
Thane shall erthe of erthe hafe a foulle stinke.

9a_____

Have pity, pity, friends, have pity on me,
  Thus much at least, may it please you, of your grace!
I lie not under hazel or hawthorn-tree
  Down in this dungeon ditch, mine exile's place
  By leave of God and fortune's foul disgrace.
Girls, lovers, glad young folk and newly wed,
Jumpers and jugglers, tumbling heel o'er head,
  Swift as a dart, and sharp as needle-ware,
Throats clear as bells that ring the kine to shed,
  Your poor old friend, what, will you leave him there?

Singers that sing at pleasure, lawlessly,
  Light, laughing, gay of word and deed, that race
And run like folk light-witted as ye be
  And have in hand nor curren coin nor base,
  Ye wait too long, for now he's dying apace.
Rhymes of lays and roundels sung and read
Ye'll brew him broth too late when he lies dead.
  Nor wind nor lightning, sunbeam nor fresh air,
May pierce the thick wall's bound where lies his bed;
  Your poor old friend, what, will you leave him there?

O noble folk from tithes and taxes free,
  Come and behold him in this piteous case,
Ye that nor king nor emperor holds in fee,
  But only God in heaven; behold his face
  Who needs must fast, Sundays and holidays,
Which makes his teeth like rakes; and when he hath fed
With never a cake for banquet but dry bread,
  Must drench his bowels with much cold watery fare,
With board nor stool, but low on earth instead.
  Your poor old friend, what, will you leave him there?

Princes afore-named, old and young foresaid,
Get me the king's seal and my pardon sped,
  And hoist me in some basket up with care:

15

So swine will help each other ill bested,
For where one squeaks they run in leaps ahead.
    Your poor old friend, what, will you leave him there?

9b_____

Some tyme this world was so stedfast and stable
That mannes word was obligacioun
And now hit is so fals and deceivable,
That word and deed, as in conclusion,
Ben nothyng oon, for turned up so doun
Is al this world throgh mede and wilfulnesse,
That al is lost for lak of stedfastnesse.

What maketh this world to be so variable,
But lust that folk have in dissensioun?
Among us now a man is holde unable,
But if he can, by some collusion,
Don his neighbour wrong or oppressioun.
What causeth this, but wilful wrecchednesse,
That al is lost, for lak of stedfastnesse?

Trouthe is put doun, resoun is holden fable;
Vertu hath now no dominacioun,
Pitee exyled, no man is merciable.
Through covetyse is blent discrecioun;
The world hath mad a permutacioun
Fro right to wrong, fro trouthe to fikelnesse,
That al is lost, for lak of stedfastnesse.

        L'Envoy to King Richard.
O prince, desire to be honourable
Cherish thy folk and hate extorcioun!
Suffre no thyng, that may be reprevable
To thyn estat, don in thy regioun.
Shew forth thy swerd of castigacioun,
Dred God, do law, love trouthe and worthynesse
And wed thy folk ageyn to stedfastnesse.

16

10a_____

They fle from me, that sometyme did me seke
With naked fote, stalking in my chambr.
I have sene thaim gentill, tame and meke,
That now are wyld, and do not remember
That sometime they put theimself in daunger
To take bread at my hand; and now they raunge
Besely seking with a continuell change.

Thanked be fortune it hath been othrewise
Twenty tymes better; but once in speciall
In thin arraye, after a pleasaunt gyse
When her loose gowne from her shoulders did fall,
And she me caught in her arms long and small
Therewith all sweetly did me kysse
And softely said: "Dere herte howe like you this?"

It was no dreme: I lay brode waking
But all is torned, thorough my gentilness
Into a straunge fasshion of forsaking;
And I have leve to goo of her goodenes:
And she also to use new fangilnes;
But syns that I so kyndely am served,
I wold fain knowe what she hath deserved.

10b_____

The long love that in my thought doth harbor,
And in my heart doth keep his residence,
Into my face presseth with bold pretense
And there encampeth, spreading his banner.
She that me learns to love and suffer
And wills that my trust and lust's negligence
Be reined by reason, shame and reverence
With his hardiness takes displeasure.
Wherewithal unto the heart's forest he flieth,
Leaving his enterprise with pain and cry,

17

And there him hideth, and not appeareth.
What may I do, when my master feareth,
But in the field with him to live and die?
For good is the life ending faithfully.

11a_____

'Though your clothes are of light Lincolne green
     And mine gray russett and torne,
Yet it doth not you beseeme
     To doe an old man scorne.'

'I scorne thee not, old man,' says Robin,
     'By the faith of my body;
Doe off thy clothes, thou shalt haue mine,
     For it may noe better bee.'

But Robin did on this old mans hose,
     The were torne in the wrist;
'When I looke on my leggs,' said Robin,
     'Then for to laugh I list.'

But Robin did on the old mans shooes
     And the were cliit full cleane;
'Now by my faith,' says Little John,
     'These are good for thornes keene.'

But Robin did on the old mans cloake,
     And it was torne in the necke;
'Now by my faith,' said William Scarlett,
     'Heere shold be set a specke.'

But Robin did on this old mans hood,
     Itt gogled on his crown;
'When I come into Nottingham,' said Robin,
     'My hood it will lightly downe.

'But yonder is an outwood,' said Robin,
     'An outwood all and a shade,
And thither I reede you, may merrymen all
     The ready way to take.'

11b_____

'But bend your bowes, and stroke your strings
     Set the gallow-tree aboute,

And Christs cursse on his heart,' said Robin,
    'That spares the sheriffe and the sergiant!'

When the sheriffe see gentle Robin wold shoote
    He held up both his hands;
Sayes, Aske, good Robin, and thou shalt haue
    Whether it be house or land.

'I will neither have house nor land,' said Robin,
    Nor gold, nor none of thy ffee,
But I will haue those three squires
    To the greene fforest with me.'

'Now marry, Gods forbott,' said the sheriffe,
    'That ever that shold bee
For why, they be the kings ffelons,
    They are all condemned to dye.'

'But grant me my askinge,' said Robin,
    Or by the faith of my body
Thou shalt be the first man
    Shall flower this gallow-tree.'

12a_____

Dark night, that from the eye his function takes,
The ear more quick of apprehension makes;
Wherein it doth impair the seeing sense,
It pays the hearing double recompense.
Thou art not by mine eye, Lysander, found;
Mine ear, I thank it, brought me to thy sound.
But why unkindly didst thou leave me so?

12b_____

Puppet? Why so? Ay, that way goes the game.
Now I perceive that she hath made compare
Between our statures; she hath urged her height;
And with her personage, her tall personage,
Her height, forsooth, she had prevailed with him.
And are you grown so high in his esteem
Because I am so dwarfish and so low?
How low am I, thou painted maypole? Speak;
How low am I? I am not yet so low
But that my nails can reach unto thine eyes.

12c_____

Here, take this purse, thou whom the heavens' plagues
Have humbled to all strokes: that I am wretched
Makes thee happier. Heavens, deal so still!
Let the superfluous and lust-dieted man,
That slaves your ordinance, that will not see
Because he doth not feel, feel your power quickly;
So distribution should undo excess
And each man have enough.

13a_____

Here the anthem doth commence:
Love and constancy is dead;
Phoenix and the turtle fled
In a mutual flame from hence.

So they loved, as love in twain
Had the essence but in one;
Two distincts, division none:
Number there in love was slain.

Hearts remote, yet not asunder;
Distance, and no space was seen
'Twixt the turtle and his queen:
But in them it were a wonder.

So between them love did shine,
That the turtle saw his right
Flaming in the phoenix' sight;
Either was the other's mine.

Property was thus appalled
That the self was not the same;
Single nature's double name
Neither two nor one was called.

Reason, in itself confounded,
Saw division grow together,
To themselves yet either neither,
Simple were so well compounded;

That it cried, How true a twain
Seemeth this concordant one!
Love hath reason, reason none,
If what parts can so remain.

Whereupon it made this threne
To the phoenix and the dove,
Co-supremes and stars of love,
As chorus to their tragic scene.

13b_____

But he, though blind of sight,
Despised and thought extinguisht quite,
With inward eyes illuminated,
His fiery virtue roused
From under ashes into sudden flame,
And as an ev'ning dragon came,
Assailant on the perchèd roosts,
And nests in order ranged,
Of tame villatic fowl; but as an eagle
His cloudless thunder bolted on their heads.
So virtue, giv'n for lost,
Deprest and overthrown, as seemed,
Like that self-begott'n bird
In the Arabian woods embost,
That no second knows nor third,
And lay erewhile a holocaust,
From out her ashy womb now teemed,
Revives, reflourishes, then vigorous most
When most unactive deemed;
And though her body die, her fame survives,
A secular bird, ages of lives.

14a_____

Where like a pillow on a bed,
    A Pregnant bank swell'd up, to rest
The violets reclining head,
    Sat we two, one another's best.
Our hands were firmly cemented
    With a fast balm, which thence did spring,
Our eye-beams twisted and did thread
    Our eyes, upon one double string;
So to'entergraft our hands, as yet
    Was all the means to make us one,
And pictures in our eyes to get
    Was all our propagation.
As 'twixt two equall Armies, Fate
    Suspends uncertaine victorie,
Our souls, (which to advance their state,
    Were gone out,) hung 'twixt her, and me.
And whilst our souls negotiate there,
    We like sepulchral statues lay;
All day, the same our postures were,
    And we said nothing all the day.
If any, so by love refin'd
    That he soul's language understood
And by good love were grown all mind,
    Within convenient distance stood,
He (though he knew not which soul spake
    Because both meant, both spoke the same)
Might thence a new concoction take
    And part far purer than he came.
This ecstasy doth unperplex
    (We said) and tell us what we love,
We see by this, it was not sex
    We see, we saw not what did move:
But as all several souls contain
    Mixture of things they know not what,
Love these mixed souls, doth mix again
    And make both one, each this and that.

14b_____

A single violet transplant,
    The strength, the colour and the size,
(All which before was poore, and scant,)
    Redoubles still, and multiplies.
When love, with one another so
    Interanimates two souls,
That abler soul, which thence doth flow
    Defects of loneliness controls.
We then, who are this new soul, know,
    Of what we are compos'd and made,
For, th' Atomies of which we grow
    Are souls whom no change can invade.
But O alas, so long, so far
    Our bodies why do we forbear?
They are ours, though they are not we, We are
    The intelligences, they the sphere.
We owe them thanks, because they thus,
    Did us, to us, at first convey;
Yielded their forces, sense, to us,
    Nor are dross to us, but allay.
On man heaven's influence works not so
    But that it first imprints the ayre,
So soul into the soul may flow
    Though it to body first repair.
As our blood labours to beget
    Spirits, as like souls as it can,
Because such fingers need to knit
    That subtile knot, which makes us man:
So must pure lovers' souls descend
    T' affections, and to faculties,
Which sense may reach and apprehend,
    Else a great Prince in prison lies.
To'our bodies turn we then, that so
    Weak men on love reveal'd may look;

Loves mysteries in souls do grow
    But yet the body is his book.
And if some lover, such as we,
    Have heard this dialogue of one,
Let him still mark us, he shall see
    Small change, when we'are to bodies gone.

15a_____

Hic jacet John Shorthose
Sine hose, sine shoes, sine breeches;
Qui fuit, dum vixit,
Sine goods, sine lands, sine riches.

15b_____

As lightning or a taper's light,
Thine eyes, and not thy voice, waked me;
        Yet I thought thee
(For thou lovest truth) an Angell, at first sight,
But when I saw thou sawest my heart,
And knew'st my thoughts, beyond an Angel's art,
When thou knew'st what I dreamt, when thou knew'st when
Excesse of joy would wake me, and cam'st then,
I must confesse, it could not choose but be
Profane to think thee anything but thee.

15c_____

Hang all officers, we cry
And the magistrate too, by!
When the subsidy's increased
We are not a penny sessed;
Nor will any go to law,
With the beggar for a straw.
All which happiness, he brags,
He doth owe unto his rags.

16a_____

Fair daffadils, we weep to see
    You haste away so soon:
As yet the early-rising sun
    Has not attained his noon.
           Stay, stay
    Until the hasting day
           Has run
    But to the evensong,
And, having prayed together, we
    Will go with you along.

We have short time to stay as you;
    We have as short a spring,
As quick a growth to meet decay,
    As you or anything.
           We die
    As your hours do, and dry
           Away
    Like to the summer's rain,
Or as the pearls of morning's dew,
    Ne'er to be found again.

16b_____

When a daffadil I see
Hanging down his head t'wards me,
Guess I may what I must be:
First, I shall decline my head;
Secondly, I shall be dead;
Lastly, safely buried.

16c_____

Little wrists,
Is your content
My sight or hold,
Or your small air
That lights and trysts?

Red alder berry
Will singly break;
But you — how slight — do:
So that even
A lover exists.

17a_____

Great Negative! how vainly would the wise
Inquire, define, distinguish, teach, devise?
Didst thou not stand to point their dull philosophies.

Is, or *is not* the two great ends of Fate
And, true or false, the subject of debate,
That perfect or destroy the vast designs of Fate;

When they have rack'd the politician's breast,
Within thy bosom most securely rest,
And, when reduc'd to thee, are least unsafe and best.

But Nothing, why does Something still permit,
That sacred monarchs should at council sit,
With persons highly thought at best for nothing fit?

Whilst weighty Something modestly abstains
From princes' coffers, and from statesman's brains,
And nothing there like stately Nothing reigns.

Nothing, who dwell'st with fools in grave disguise,
For whom they reverend shapes and forms devise,
Lawn sleeves, and furs, and gowns, when they like thee look
    wise.

French truth, Dutch prowess, British policy,
Hibernian learning, Scotch civility,
Spaniards' dispatch, Danes' wit, are mainly seen in thee.

The great man's gratitude to his best friend,
Kings' promises, whores vows, towards thee they bend,
Flow swiftly into thee, and in thee ever end.

17b_____

The Grape that can with Logic absolute
The Two-and-Seventy jarring Sects confute:
    The subtle Alchemist that in a Trice
Life's leaden Metal into Gold transmute.

For in and out, above, about, below
'Tis nothing but a Magic Shadow-show,
  Play'd in a Box whose Candle is the Sun,
Round which we Phantom Figures come and go.

And if the Wine you drink, the Lip you press,
End in the Nothing all Things end in — Yes —
  Then fancy while Thou art, Thou art but what
Thou shalt be — Nothing — Thou shalt not be less.

17c_____

And God-appointed Berkeley that proved all things a dream,
That this pragmatical preposterous pig of a world,
  its farrow that so solid seem
Must vanish on the instant if the mind but change its theme,

Saeva Indignatio and the labourer's hire
The strength that gives our blood and state magnanimity of its
  own desire
Everything that is not God consumed with intellectual fire.

18a

Lo! yonder shed; observe its garden-ground
With the low paling, form'd of wreck, around:
There dwells a fisher; if you view his boat,
With bed and barrel 't is his house afloat;
Look at his house, where ropes, nets, blocks, abound,
Tar, pitch, and oakum — 't is his boat aground:
That space enclosed, but little he regards,
Spread o'er with relics of masts, sails, and yards:
Fish by the wall, on spit of elder, rest,
Of all his food, the cheapest and the best,
By his own labour caught, for his own hunger dress'd.

Here our reformers come not; none object
To paths polluted, or upbraid neglect;
None care that ashy heaps at doors are cast,
That coal-dust flies along the blinding blast:
None heed the stagnant pools on either side,
Where new-launch'd ships of infant sailors ride:

18b

He voyd of feare made aunswere thus, Acetis is my name:
Of Parentes but of lowe degree in Lidy land I came.
No ground for painfull Oxe to till, no sheepe to bear me wooll
My father left me: no nor Horse, nor Asse, nor Cow nor Bool.
God wote he was but poore himselfe, With line and bayted hooke
The frisking fishes in the pooles upon his Reede he tooke.
His handes did serve instead of landes, his substance was his
    craft.
Now have I made you true accompt of all that he me laft,
As well of ryches as of trades, in which I was his heire
And successour. For when that death bereft him use of aire
Save water he me nothing left. It is the thing alone
Which for my lawfull heritage I clayme, and other none.
Soone after I (bicause that loth I was to ay abide
In that poore state) did learne a ship by cunning hande to guide
And for to know the raynie signe . . .

With all the dwellings of the winds that made the seas so rough
And eke such Havens as are meet to harbrough vessels in,
With everie starre and heavenly signs that guides to shipmen bin.

19a_____

Hear me, auld Hangie, for a wee
An' let poor damned bodies be;
I'm sure sma' pleasure it can gie,
    E'n to a deil,
To skelp an' scaud poor dogs like me,
    An' hear us squeel!

Lang syne, in Eden's bonnie yard,
When youthfu' lovers first were pair'd,
And all the soul of love they shared,
    The raptured hour,
Sweet on the fragrant, flowery swaird
    In shady bower:

Then you, ye auld sneak-drawing dog!
Ye come to Paradise *incog.,*
An' play'd on man a cursed brogue
    (Black be your fa!)
And gied the infant warld a shog,
    'Maist ruin'd a'

And now, auld Cloots, I ken ye're thinkin'
A certain Bardie 's rantin', drinkin',
Some luckless hour will send him linkin',
    To your black pit;
But faith! He'll turn a corner jinkin'
    And cheat you yet.

19b_____

What was I, or my generation,
That I should get such exaltation,
I wha deserve sic just damnation
    For broken laws,
Five thousand years 'fore my creation,
    Through Adam's cause!

When frae my mither's womb I fell
Thou might hae plungèd me in hell,
To gnash my gums, to weep and wail,
    In burnin' lake,
Where damnèd devils roar and yell,
    Chain'd to a stake.

Yet I am here, a chosen sample,
To show thy grace is great and ample;
I'm here a pillar in thy temple,
    Strong as a rock,
A guide, a buckler, and example
    To a' thy flock.

Lord! mind Gawn Hamilton's deserts,
He drinks, and swears, and playes at cartes,
Yet has sae mony takin' arts,
    Wi' grit and sma'
Frae God's ain preists and people's hearts
    He steals awa'

And when we chasten'd him therefor,
Thou kens how he bred sic a splore,
And set the warld in a roar
    O' laughin at us:
Curse thou his basket and his store,
    Kail and potatoes.

But, Lord, remember me and mine
Wi' mercies temporal and divine,
That I for gear and grace may shine,
    Excell'd by nane,
And a' the glory shall be thine.

20a_____

The tears into his eyes were brought,
    And thanks and praises seem'd to run
So fast out of his heart, I thought
    They never would have done.
— I've heard of hearts unkind, kind deeds
    With coldness still returning;
Alas! the gratitude of men
    Hath oftener left me mourning.

20b_____

O waly, waly, up the bank,
    O waly, waly, doun the brae,
And waly, waly, yon burn-side,
    Where I and my love were wont to gae!
I lean'd my back unto an aik,
    I thocht it was a trustie tree,
But first it bow'd and syne it brak', —
    Sae my true love did lichtlie me.

O waly, waly, but love be bonnie
    A little time while it is new!
But when it's auld it waxeth cauld,
    And fadeth awa' like the morning dew.
O wherefore should I busk my heid,
    Or wherefore should I kame my hair?
For my true love has me forsook,
    And says he'll never lo'e me mair.

Noo Arthur's Seat sall be my bed,
    The sheets sall ne'er be press'd by me;
Saint Anton's well sall be my drink;
    Since my true love's forsaken me.
Martinmas wind, when wilt thou blaw,
    And shake the green leaves off the tree?
O gentle death, when wilt thou come?
    For of my life I am wearie.

'Tis not the frost that freezes fell,
    Nor blawing snaw's inclemencie,
'Tis not sic cauld that makes me cry;
    But my love's heart grown cauld to me.
When we cam' in by Glasgow toun,
    We were a comely sicht to see;
My love was clad in the black velvet,
    An' I mysel' in cramasie.

But had I wist before I kiss'd
    That love had been so ill to win,
I'd lock'd my heart in a case o' goud,
    And pinn'd it wi' a siller pin.
Oh, oh! if my young babe were born,
    And set upon the nurse's knee;
And I mysel' were dead and gane,
    And the green grass growing over me!

20c_____

When my mother died I was very young,
And my father sold me while yet my tongue,
Could scarcely cry, ' 'Weep, 'weep! 'weep! 'weep!'
So your chimneys I sweep, and in soot I sleep.

20d_____

And thou — who tell'st me to forget,
Thy looks are wan, thine eyes are wet.

21a_____

Dusk winding-stairs, dim galleries got past,
You gain the inmost chambers, gain at last
A maple-panelled room: that haze which seems
Floating about the panel, if there gleams
A sunbeam over it, will turn to gold
And in light-graven characters unfold
The Arab's wisdom everywhere; what shade
Marred them a moment, those slim pillars made,
Cut like a company of palms to prop
The roof, each kissing top entwined with top,
Leaning together; in the carver's mind
Some knot of bacchanals, flushed cheek combined
With straining forehead, shoulders purpled, hair
Diffused between, who in a goat-skin bear
A vintage; graceful sister-palms!

21b_____

Thought clambers up,
snail like, upon the wet rocks
hidden from sun and sight —
hedged in by the pouring torrent —
and has its birth and death there
in that moist chamber, shut from
the world — and unknown to the world,
cloaks itself in mystery —

22a_____

Give her but a least excuse to love me!
When — where —
How — can this arm establish her above me,
If fortune fixed her as my lady there,
There already, to eternally reprove me?
("Hist" — said Kate the Queen;
But "Oh" cried the maiden, binding her tresses;
" 'Tis only a page that carols unseen
Crumbling your hounds their messes!")

22b_____

Come with bows bent and with emptying of quivers
    Maiden most perfect, lady of light,
With a noise of winds and many rivers,
    With a clamour of waters and with might;
Bind on thy sandals, O thou most fleet,
Over the splendour and speed of thy feet;
For the faint east quickens, the wan west shivers,
    Round the feet of the day and the feet of the night.

22c_____

    Lassie wi' the lint-white locks,
    Bonnie lassie, artless lassie,
    Wilt thou wi' me tent the flocks,
    Wilt thou be my dearie O?

When Cynthia lights, wi' silver ray,
The weary shearer's hameward way;
Through yellow waving fields we'll stray,
    And talk o' love, my dearie O!

22d_____

Hot sunne, coole fire, tempered with sweet aire
Black shade, fair nurse, shadow my white haire

Shine sun, burne fire, breathe aire, and ease mee,
Black shade, fair nurse, shroud me and please me
Shadow (my sweet nurse) keep me from burning
Make not my glad cause, cause of mourning.
Let not my beauties fire
Enflame unstaied desire,
Nor pierce any bright eye
That wandreth lightly.

22e_____

You'll love me yet! — and I can tarry
    Your love's protracted growing:
June reared that bunch of flowers you carry,
    From seeds of April's sowing.

I plant a heartfull now: some seed
    At least is sure to strike,
And yield — what you'll not pluck indeed,
    Not love, but, maybe, like.

You'll look at least on love's remains,
    A grave's one violet
Your look? — that pays a thousand pains.
    What's death? You'll love me yet!

23a_____

Hedge-crickets sing;

23b_____

Love, of this clearest, frailest glass
Divide the properties, so as
In the division may appear
Clearness for me, frailty for her.

23c_____

Fair glass of light, I love you, and could still,
Were not this glorious casket stored with ill:
But I must tell you, now my thoughts revolt;
For he's no man on whom perfections wait
That, knowing sin within, will touch the gate.
You are a fair viol and your sense the strings,
Who, finger'd to make man his lawful music,
Would draw heaven down and all the gods, to hearken,
But being play'd upon before your time,
Hell only danceth at so harsh a chime.

23d_____

There's a better shine
on the pendulum
than is on my hair
and many times
    •   •   •   •
I've seen it there.

41

24a_____

Tagus, farewell, that westward with thy streams
Turns up the grains of gold already tried;
With spur and sail for I go seek the Thames,
Gainward the sun, that showeth her wealthy pride;
And to the town that Brutus sought by dreams,
Like bended moon doth lend her lusty side,
My king, my country, alone for whom I live —
O mighty Love, the wings for this me give!

24b_____

Tyre, I now look from thee then, and to Tarsus
Intend my travel, where I'll hear from thee;
And by whose letters I'll dispose myself.
The care I had and have of subjects' good
On thee I lay, whose wisdom's strength can bear it.
I'll take thy word for faith, not ask thine oath:
Who shuns not to break one will sure crack both:
But in our orbs we'll live so round and safe,
That time of both this truth shall ne'er convince,
Thou show'dst a subject's shine, I a true prince.

25a——————

Say, darkeys, hab you seen de massa,
    Wid de muffstash on he face,
Go long de road some time dis mornin',
    Like he gwine leabe de place?
He see de smoke way up de ribber
    Whar de Lincum gunboats lay;
He took he hat an' leff berry sudden,
    And I spose he's runned away.
        De massa run? ha! ha!
        De darkey stay? ho, ho!
        It mus' be now de kingdum comin',
        An' de yar ob Jubilo.

He six foot one way, two feet tudder,
    And he weighs tree hundred pounds,
His coat so big he couldn't pay de tailor,
    And it won't go half way round.
He drill so much dey call him Cap'an,
    An' he get so drefful tann'd,
I spec he try an' fool dem Yankees
    For to tink he's contraband.
        De massa run? ha! ha!
        De darkey stay? ho! ho!
        It mus' be now de kingdum comin',
        An de year ob Jubilo!

25b——————

Lollai, lollai, litil child
    Whi wepistou so sore?
Nedis mostou wepe
    Hit was iyarkid the yore
Ever to lib in sorow,
    And sich and mourne evere,
As thin eldren did er this,
    Whil hi alives were.

> Lollai, lollai, litil child,
> > Child, lollai, lullow!
> Into uncuth world
> > Icommen so ertow.

25c_____

In going to my naked bed as one that would have slept,
I heard a wife sing to her child, that long before had wept;
She sighèd sore and sang full sweet, to bring the babe to rest,
That would not cease but crièd still, in sucking at her breast.
She was full weary of her watch, and grievèd with her child,
She rockèd it and rated it, till that on her it smiled.
Then did she say, Now have I found this proverb true to prove,
The falling out of faithful friends renewing is of love.

She said that neither king nor prince nor lord could live aright,
Until their puissance they did prove, their manhood and their
    might.
When manhood shall be matched so that fear can take no place,
Then weary works make warriors each other to embrace,
And left their force that failèd them, which did consume the
    rout,
That might before have lived their time, their strength and
    nature out:
Then did she sing as one that thought no man could her reprove,
The falling out of faithful friends renewing is of love.

PART II

MORE COMPARISONS — and CONSIDERATIONS

" . . . only the primarily beautiful and new (old: new) re-
maining."

WILLIAM CARLOS WILLIAMS

"You will find many pencil marks, for I made them as I read.
I let them stand, for though many receive their answer as the
story proceeds, yet they show how the wording impresses a mind
fresh to the subject, and perhaps here and there you may like to
alter it slightly, if you wish the full idea, i.e. not an inaccurate
one, to be suggested at first; and yet after all I believe it is not
your exposition, but the natural jumping to a conclusion that
affects or has affected my pencil."

MICHAEL FARADAY

The lasting attractions in the words of a poem and its construction make it classic and contemporary at the same time.
The critical matter following the samples develops this statement. Illustrations given are assumed, for the most part, to be
good; the few said to be poor serve merely as contrast.

1a_____

There sat the seniors of the Trojan race
(Old Priam's chiefs, and most in Priam's grace . . .
Antenor grave, and sage Ucalegon
Lean'd on the walls, and bask'd before the sun . . .
Chiefs, who no more in bloody fights engage,
In summer days like grasshoppers rejoice,
A bloodless race, that send a feeble voice.
These, when the Spartan Queen approach'd the tower
In secret own'd resistless Beauty's power:
They cried 'No wonder, such celestial charms
For nine long years have set the world in arms!
What winning graces! What majestic mien!
She moves a Goddess, and she looks a Queen.
Yet hence, oh Heav'n! convey that fatal face
And from destruction save the Trojan race.

> Homer, *Iliad*, Bk. III
> translated by Alexander Pope
> 1715

1b_____

Virgins and boys, mid-age and wrinkled eld,
Soft infancy, that nothing can but cry,
Add to my clamour! Let us pay betimes
A moiety of that mass of moan to come.
Cry, Troyans, cry! Practise your eyes with tears!
Troy must not be, nor goodly Ilion stand.
Our firebrand brother, Paris, burns us all.
Cry, Troyans, cry! A Helen and a woe!
Cry, cry! Troy burns, or else let Helen go.

> William Shakespeare
> *Troilus and Cressida*, II, ii
> 1602

COMMENT:

1a: A translation of Homer. 1b: Shakespeare's inter-
pretation of Homer's story. The early epic was concerned with

telling a story. Homer is the master of the art of narrative in verse. He is also master of certain *musical* effects of verse — such as, rendering the sound of things by the sound of words and the tempo of action by the tempo of words.

Translators or adaptors have to find an equivalent in English for the Greek of these things. The emotional drive must be retained. 1a is clipped verse but the emotion of speech and music have been lost.

NOTE:

A simple order of speech is an asset in poetry.

2a_____

First came my soldier Elpenor's spirit
    Which left the body just when we set sail,
So that we had no leisure to inter it;
    His heavy fate I did with tears bewail.
How now, quoth I, Elpenor? art thou here
    Already? Couldst thou me so much outstrip?
I first came forth, and left thee in the rear
    Hast thou on foot outgone my good black ship?
Then said Elpenor: Issue of Jove, divine
    Ulysses, I had come along with th' bark,
But the Devil and excess of wine
    Made me to fall, and break my neck i' th' dark.
I went to bed late by a ladder steep
    At top o' th' house the room was where I lay,
Wak'd at the noise of parting, half asleep,
    Headlong I hither came, the nearest way.

Homer, *The Odyssey*, Bk. XI
translated by Thomas Hobbes
c. 1673 - 1677

2b_____

But the first that drew anigh me was our friend Elpenor's shade
For as yet he was not buried beneath the Earth wide-wayed;
We had left his body unburied, unwept, in Circe's hall,
Since other need and labour on our fellowship did fall.
So I wept when I beheld him and was sorry for his sake,
And I sent my voice unto him and a wingèd word I spake:
"How camest thou, Elpenor, beneath the dusk and the dark?
And swifter afoot has thou wended than I in my coal-black
    bark."
God's doom and wine unstinted on me the bane had brought
I lay in the house of Circe and waking had no thought
To get me back and adown by the way of the ladders tall:
But downright from the roof I tumbled, and brake my neck
    withal

From the backbone, and unto Hades and his house my soul must fare.

> Homer, *The Odyssey*, Bk. XI
> translated by William Morris
> 1897

COMMENT:

2a: A translation of Homer. 2b: Another translation of the same passage. Both are poor examples of poetry. The Hobbes is very ordinary, very prosaic. The Morris is naive. The cradling lullaby of the verse and the monotonous stopping of the rhymes are very tiring. Morris *pads* his lines — that is, uses needless words to fill out his meter. It can at least be said of the Hobbes that it occasionally *reads* for the simple sense of the story.

Morris uses three circumlocutions in every line, and, in 1897, over 200 years after Hobbes, writes an English which is less the straight order of English speech than Hobbes'. *Winged word, coal-black bark* are aimless striving for effective description. They do not convey Homer. Morris writes *I sent my voice unto him*, for *I said to him*. He is piling it on thin when he adds *and a winged word I spake!*

NOTE:

Prose chopped up into "verses" of alternately rhyming lines of an equal number of syllables is not poetry. A good poet never uses a word unless it adds to the meaning of the thing said. A good poet writing in English usually writes good English, unless the nature of his subject matter compels otherwise.

The music of verse carries an emotional quality; when the music slackens, emotion dissipates, and the poetry is poor.

3a_____

Gold from the earth in steade of fruits we pluck,
Soldiers by blood to be inricht have luck.
Courts shut the poore out; wealth gives estimation.
Thence grows the Judge, and knight of reputation.
All they possess: they governe fields, and lawes,
They manadge peace, and raw warres bloody jawes,
Onely our loves let not such rich churles gaine —

> Ovid, *Elegies*, Bk. III, 8
> translated by Christopher Marlowe
> c. 1590

3b_____

Year chases year, decay pursues decay.
Still drops some joy from with'ring life away;
New forms arise, and different views engage,
Superfluous lags the vet'ran on the stage,
Till pitying nature signs the last release
And bids afflicted worth retire to peace.

> Samuel Johnson
> *The Vanity of Human Wishes*
> 1749

COMMENT:

A contrast in the effect of the use of the definite word (3a) as against the stylized word (3b) on the emotional form or content of poetry. The Marlowe is youthful work, but has more poetic fervor than the socially sophisticated versifying of the Johnson. Marlowe deals with definite things, definite occurrences, definite actions. Johnson implicitly approaches definite happenings, but removes from them living emotional richness. He dresses them in a code of social abstraction peculiar to the literary fashion of his day. Marlowe's concrete data, *Courts shut the poore out; wealth gives estimation,* and Johnson's vague code, *afflicted worth,* represent opposed poetic styles. Prof. Saintsbury has referred to the Johnson as "almost a great poem, and beyond all questions a great piece of literature, gorgeous declamation, verse-eloquence." A distinction seems to have been made between a great piece of literature and a great poem.

NOTE:

Different attitudes towards things and events are at the base of different poetic content. The definite language of Marlowe allies itself with song, one of the mainsprings of poetry. The abstract language of Johnson, though the skeleton of his verse (the heroic couplet) is the same as Marlowe's, allies itself with oratory, usually a division of the art of persuasion.

Poetry convinces not by argument but by the *form* it creates to carry its content.

4a_____

On his bow-back he hath a battle set
Of bristly pikes, that ever threat his foes;
His eyes like glow-worms, shine when he doth fret;
His snout digs sepulchres where'er he goes;
    Being moved, he strikes whate'er is in his way
    And whom he strikes his crooked tushes slay.

His brawny sides, with hairy bristles armed,
Are better proof than thy spear's point can enter;
His short thick neck cannot be easily harmed;
Being ireful, on the lion he will venture:
    The thorny brambles and embracing bushes,
    As fearful of him, part; through whom he rushes.
                    William Shakespeare
                    Venus and Adonis
                    1593

4b_____

His eies did glister blud and fire; right dreadfull was to see
His brawned necke, right dredfull was his haire which grew as
    thicke
With pricking points as one of them could well by other sticke.
And like a front of armed Pikes set close in battell ray
The sturdie bristles on his back stoode staring up alway.
Such lightning flashed from his chappes, as seared up the grasse
Now trampled he the spindling corne to ground where he did
    passe,
Now ramping up their riped hope he made the Plowman weepe.
And chankt the kernell in the eare. In vaine their floores they
    sweepe:
In vaine their Barnes for Harvest long the likely store they
    keepe.
The spreaded Vines with clustered Grapes to ground he rudely
    sent
And full of Berries loden boughes from Olife trees he rent!
On cattell also did he rage. The shepherd nor his dog,

Nor yet the Bulles could save the herdes from outrage of this Hog.
> Ovid, *Metamorphoses,* Bk. VIII
> translated by Arthur Golding
> 1565

COMMENT:

Similar subject matter — two descriptions of a wild-boar. Both are excellent verse — definite as to what they see, unified and compact as movement.

While Golding's spelling is archaic (i.e. of 1565), his English is, with rare exceptions, *modern* English. This is not surprising. Bad poets, writing apart from living English speech, have been archaic at various times, from 1300 till the present day, because they have had nothing to offer but quaintness. Good poets wrote modern English — that is, virtually, the order of speech common today — even 200 years before Golding.

The Golding written 28 years before the Shakespeare SEES MORE than the Shakespeare. The Ovid-Golding wild-boar registers the social and economic scene *besides* his merely physical presence. Shakespeare "cribbed" from Golding's Ovid certain excellences of description, but omitted a great deal which did not concern the rather pretty story of his *Venus and Adonis.*

NOTE:

Great poets are implicitly good critics of poetry. Their good work proves it. Shakespeare evidently admired Golding enough to "copy" him. Golding may not be generally known, but that he is not is perhaps the fault of lesser critics than Shakespeare.

A poet's matter should be criticized for what he intended to present, rather than for what he did not intend to present. One should distinguish, however, between a poet who writes perfectly about one detail, and another who writes perfectly about the same detail and a host of other detail covering a phase of civilization.

5a_____

Ah! Lesbia! though 'tis death to me,
I cannot choose but look on thee;
But, at the sight, my senses fly,
I needs must gaze, but, gazing, die;
Whilst trembling with a thousand fears,
Parch'd to the throat my tongue adheres,
My pulse beats quick, my breath heaves short,
My limbs deny their slight support;
Cold dews my pallid face o'erspread,
With deadly languor droops my head,
My ears with tingling echoes ring,
And life itself is on the wing,
My eyes refuse the cheering light,
Their orbs are veil'd in starless night:
Such pangs my nature sinks beneath,
And feels a temporary death.

> Catullus, *Ad Lesbiam*
> translated by Lord Byron
> 1807

5b_____

My muse, what ails this ardour?
Mine eyes be dim, my limbs shake,
My voice is hoarse, my throat scorched
My tongue to this my roof cleaves
My fancy amazed, my thoughts dulled
My heart doth ache, my life faints
My soul begins to take leave.

> Catullus, *Ad Lesbiam*
> translated by Sir Phillip Sidney
> c. 1579

COMMENT:

Two translations of Catullus whose Latin poem is a translation from the Greek of Sappho.

Table:
> Sappho — 700 B.C.
> Catullus — 87-54 (?) B.C.
> Sir Philip Sidney — 1579
> Byron — 1807

The table covers a period of 2500 years. Evidently there must be some living poetic matter in the poem of Sappho which has attracted the attention of other poets. Despite the fact that languages and mere fashions of poetic style were once in use and have fallen into disuse.

In English, one can get at this matter of Sappho through 5b better than through 5a which is a juvenile "try at it." Sidney says in 46 words what Byron in 104 says badly. He evades the monotonous regularity of line and the jingle of rhymes found in the Byron. Sidney conveys sense with a rush, to let the pulse of emotion control the beat of the words and the length of the lines. He omits rhyme, as did Sappho and Catullus.

NOTE:

A valuable poetic tradition does not gather mold; it has a continuous life based on work of permanent interest (quality). This tradition involves a knowledge of more than English poetry and the English language. Not all the great poems were written in English. There are other languages.

There are all kinds of measure (metre) in verse. No measure can be bad if it is a true accompaniment of the literal and suggestive sense of the words.

6a _____

Thay umbeset the seyis [1] bustuously
Quhill [2] fra the depe till euyrye coist fast by
The huge wallis [3] weltres apon hie
Rowit at anis [4] with stormes and wyndis thre
Eurus, Nothus, and the wynd Aphricus
(Quhilk [5] Eist, South and West wyndis hate [6] with us.)
Sone eftir this of men the clamour rais [7]
The takillis [8] graffillis cabillis [9] can frate [10] and frais.
With the cloudis, heuynnys son [11] and dayis lycht
Hid and brest out of the Troianis sycht
Derknes as nycht [12] beset the see about
The firmament gan [13] rumyleyng rare and rout [14]
The skyis oft lychtned with fyry leuyn
And schortlie baith are, see and heauyn
And euery thyng manissis [15] the men to de
Schewand [16] the dede present before thare E [17].

> Virgil, *Aeneid*
> translated by Gawin Douglas
> 1512 - 13

P.S.   This is not a word game but some of the best poetry in
English (written by a Scot).   The spelling should help sound
the words.   Sounded, they make sense.   The sentence structure
is practically that of English today.

(1) seas	(2) while	(3) waves
(4) rolled at once	(5) which	(6) are called
(7) rose	(8) tackles	(9) cables
(10) crackle	(11) sun	(12) night
(13) began	(14) roar and bellow	(15) menaces
(16) showing	(17) eye	

6b _____

Thou god of this great vast, rebuke these surges,
Which wash both heaven and hell; and thou, that hast
Upon the winds command, bind them in brass,
Having called them from the deep! O, still
Thy deafening dreadful thunders; gently quench

Thy nimble sulphurous flashes! O, how, Lychorida,
How does my queen? Thou stormest venomously;
Wilt thou spit all thyself? The seaman's whistle
Is as a whisper in the ears of death,
Unheard. Lychorida!

William Shakespeare
Pericles, III, i
1609

COMMENT:

As a description of a storm at sea, the Douglas is better than
the Shakespeare. Douglas' language is more stormily resound-
ing, more unified in its movement than Shakespeare's. The
Shakespeare is obviously not mean rhetoric, but it is fanciful
and somewhat fitful in its movement, and, in suggestion, intri-
cate, though sometimes precise: *as a whisper in the ears of
death, Unheard.* Douglas has eyes and ears fastened on the sea.
Shakespeare, writing a play, concerns himself again and again
with the actor sounding his verses before an audience.

NOTE:

The sound of the words is sometimes 95% of poetic presentation. One can often appreciate the connotations of the sound
of words merely by listening, even if the language is foreign.
The Scotch of Gawin Douglas can hardly be called foreign, if
one reads English. What is foreign to poetry is the word which
means little or nothing — either as sound, image, or relation of
ideas. If, in any line of poetry, one word can be replaced by
another and "it makes no difference," that line is bad.

The technique of narrative poetry is one art; the technique
of poetic drama is another.

7a_____

When in this workes first verse I trode aloft,
Love slackt my Muse, and made my numbers soft.
I have no mistress, nor no favorit
Being fittest matter for a wanton wit.
Thus I complain'd, but love unlockt his quiver,
Tooke out the shaft, ordain'de my heart to shiver:
And bent his sinewie bowe upon his knee,
Saying, Poet heere 's a worke beseeming thee.
Oh woe is mee, hee never shootes but hits,
I burne, love in my idle bosome sits
Let my first verse be sixe, my last five feete,
Fare-well sterne warre, for blunter Poets meete.
Elegian Muse, that warblest amorous laies,
Girt my shine browe with Sea-banke Mirtle sprays.

> Ovid, *Elegies,* Bk. I, 1
> translated by Christopher Marlowe
> c. 1590

7b_____

An old wood, stands uncut of long yeares space,
Tis credible some godhead haunts the place.
In midst thereof a stone-pav'd sacred spring,
Where round about small birdes most sweetely sing.
Heere while I walke hid close in shadie grove,
To finde what worke my muse might move I strove.
Elegia came with haires perfumed sweete,
And one, I thinke, was longer of her feete.
A decent forme, thinne robe, a lovers looke,
By her footes blemish greater grace she tooke.

> Ovid, *Elegies,* Bk. III, 1
> translated by Christopher Marlowe
> c. 1590

COMMENT:

Two translations of the Latin *elegiac* (love poetry). The basic sophistication and worldliness of the Latin, the mentality of

Ovid, persist in these translations, despite the novelties of composition which the translations themselves present as English of their times.

NOTE:

Good verse is determined by the "core of the matter" — which is, after all, the poet's awareness of the differences, changes and possibilities of existence. If poetry does not always translate literally from one language to another, from one time to another, certain lasting emotions find an equivalent or paraphrase in all times. The equivalent or paraphrase, if it be done well, is poetry in its own right, not merely translation.

8a_____

Bytuene Mersh ant Averil
    When spray beginneth to springe
The lutel foul hath hire wyl
    On hyre lud [1] to synge,
    Ich libbe [2] in love-longinge
    For semlokest [3] of alle thinge;
    He [4] may me blisse bringe;
Icham in hire baundoun. [5]
    An hendy [6] hap ichabbe yhent; [7]
    Ichot from hevene it is me sent;
    From alle wymmen mi love is lent [8]
Ant lyht on Alysoun.

On heu hire her [9] is fayr ynoh,
    Hire browe broune, hire eye blake
With lossum [10] chere he on me loh, [11]
    With middel smal ant wel ymake.
    Bote [12] he me wolle to hire take,
    Forte [13] buen [13] hire owen make,
    Longe to lyven ichulle forsake,
Ant feye [14] fallen adoun.
Nihtes when I wende [15] ant wake,
    Forthi [16] myn wonges [17] waxeth won.
Levedi, [18] al for thine sake
    Longinge is ylent me on.
    In world nis [19] non so wytermon, [20]
    That al hire bounte telle con.
    Hire swyre [21] is whittore than the swon
Ant feyrest may in toune.

Icham for wowing al forwake, [22]
    Wery so water in wore. [23]
Lest eny reve me my make, [24]
    Ichabbe y-yerned yore. [25]
    Betere is tholien [26] whyle sore,
    Then mournen evermore
    Geynest [27] under gore, [28]

Herkne to my roun. (29)
> An hendy hap ichabbe yhent;
> Ichot from hevene it is me sent;
> From alle wymmen my love is lent

Ant lyht on Alysoun.

> *Alisoun,* (MS. Harleian 2253)
> Southern English Dialect,
> late 13th, early 14th centuries

(1) voice
(2) live
(3) seemliest
(4) she
(5) lordship
(6) fair
(7) gained
(8) turned
(9) hair
(10) lovesome
(11) laughed
(12) unless
(13) For to be
(14) lifeless
(15) turn
(16) (for this) therefore
(17) cheeks
(18) lady
(19) is not
(20) wise man
(21) neck
(22) spent with vigils
(23) weir
(24) mate
(25) long
(26) endure
(27) most graceful
(28) skirt
(29) song

8b_____

March is yielding to April
Leaf and flower afresh they spring,
Little birdlings at their will
In their wise do sing.
I in love and longing go
For the sweetest maid I know,
She can bring me out of woe,
I to her am bound.
A happy chance doth me betide
Methinks that Heaven my choice did guide
From other maids to turn aside,
And light on Alisoun.

> *Alisoun*
> translated by Jessie L. Weston
> in *The Chief Middle English Poets*
> 1913

COMMENT:

8a: *Alysoun,* as written c. 1300, Early Middle English. 8b: A translation into modern English of the first stanza of the same poem.

GUIDE to 8a: The sound of the words should help give their modern English meaning. The glossary explains the rare and old words. Historians of the English language have figured out how Middle English was pronounced. For the present purpose, however — reading for pleasure — the words may be pronounced as modern English, with something of brogue (perhaps "burr") in it, and with full value given to the vowels. The final *e* of words is pronounced like *e* in *water* — as the smoothness of the rhythm suggests, and at the end of lines.

NOTE:

The preceding guide plus a glossary are perhaps all the aid necessary in reading Middle English poetry. In any case, the guide and glossary given are enough to prove that 8b does *not* translate the *sound* of 8a and its specific denotations and connotations (that is, the meaning). Those interested in the accurate transmission of feeling through words — which is what the art of poetry consists of — will prefer 8a. The language and grammar of 8a are not foreign. There is only one surprising difference from modern English: the word *he* in *Alysoun* denotes *she*.

8a is more familiar speech than 8b. *From alle wymmen* (which equals *from all women*) rather than *From other maids*.

The words, lines and stanzaic structure of 8a sing better than the words, lines and stanzaic structure of 8b. That is, 8a arrives at better form of the whole poem through the detail and construction of its parts.

9a_____

I have of sorwe so gret woon [1]
That joye get I never noon,
    Now that I see my lady bright
    Which I have loved with al my might,
Is fro me deed [2] and is a-goon. [3]

Allas, deeth! [4] what ayleth thee,
That thou noldest [5] have taken me,
    Whan that thou toke my lady sweete?
That was so fayr, so fresh, so free,
So good, that men may wel see
    Of al goodnesse she had no mete. [6]

Geoffrey Chaucer
The Book of the Duchesse
1369

(1) abundance of sorrow   (2) dead   (3) gone   (4) death
(5) wouldst not take   (6) mate, equal

9b_____

Death, of thee do I make my moan,
    Who hadst my lady away from me,
    Nor wilt assuage thine enmity
Till with her life thou hast mine own:
For since that hour my strength has flown.
    Lo! what wrong was her life to thee
                        Death?

Two we were, and the heart was one;
    Which now being dead, dead I must be,
    Or seem alive as lifelessly
As in the choir the painted stone,
                        Death!

Francois Villon (c. 1431-61)
translated by D. G. Rossetti
1870

9c_____

O western wind, when wilt thou blow
That the small rain down can rain?
Christ, that my love were in my arms
    And I in my bed again!

                  Anonymous
                  c. 16th century

COMMENT:

9a and 9c are among the finest examples in English of words
written to be sung. The translation, 9b, is less singable, if at
all; i.e. the rather complex simile

    Or seem alive as lifelessly
    As in the choir the painted stone

would seem to impede the movement of any *imaginable* (certainly, *imaginative*) tune. The speaker's or singer's attention
is diverted from utterance to a kind of ornate, comparative
process.

The rhymes in 9a and 9c fall on the simple, spoken word
which is usually singable (*me, free, noon*), rather than on the
rhetorical word which, usually, is *not* singable (*moan, assuage,
painted*) ; in 9b, the voice slurs, and the mouth almost shuts
rather than opens on the word *enmity*.

9c: An example of the simplicity of folk-song rivalling mature
conscious art at its finest.

NOTE:

Simplicity of utterance and song go together. Song as
musical, poetic form is usually defined by a continuous and complete statement of the words. The fitting of words to musical
composition seems to have reached its maximum development
in English poetry as early as the 14th century. The complica-
tions of rhetorical ornament (similes, metaphors, conceits) in
later times seem to have created a printed (and worse, a
bookish) poetry written to be read silently rather than to be
spoken or sung. Effective rhyme furthers the poet's statement
and is never a stop-gap in the movement of the lines or their
meaning.

10a_____

Fra bank to bank, fra wood to wood I rin
Ourhailit with my feeble fantasie
Lik til a leaf that fallis from a tree
Or til a reed ourblowin with the wind,

Two gods guides me, the ane of them is blin,
Yea, and a bairn brocht up in vanitie,
The next a wife ingenrit of the sea
And lichter nor a dauphin with her fin.

Unhappy is the man for evermair
That tills the sand and sawis in the air,

But twice unhappier is he, I lairn
That feides in his heart a mad desire
And follows on a woman throw the fire
Led by a blind and teachit by a bairn.

Mark Alexander Boyd (1563-1601)
Sonet

10b_____

Being one day at my window all alone,
    So manie strange things happened me to see,
As much it grieveth me to thinke thereon.
At my right hand a Hynde appear'd to mee,
    So faire as mote the greatest God delite;
Two eager dogs did her pursue in chace,
Of which the one was blacke, the other white:
With deadly force so in their cruell race
    They pincht the haunches of that gentle beast,
That at the last, and in short time I spide,
Under a Rocke where she alas opprest,
Fell to the ground, and there untimely dide.
    Cruell death vanquishing so noble beautie,
    Oft makes me wayle so hard a destenie.

Edmund Spenser
The Visions of Petrarch
1590

COMMENT:

10a: Its perfection lies in the choice of the words, and in the construction of the melody which they carry: falling, first, into a division of four lines; expanding into an additional division of four; summing up their musical and emotional continuity in lines 9 and 10, which run into the final four lines — the resolution — with no let-up of emotional intensity. The imagery and verbal arrangement parallel the melodic invention by focusing interest on a contrast of sometimes two, sometimes four objects or events in a division of four lines, and by resolving them in the last six lines into the single experience of the lover composing the sonnet.

10b: The diction — the choice of words — is in many ways as beautiful as that of 10a. But the poet falls short of 10a inasmuch as his words are not always impelled by emotion and melodic invention. Dropping into pleasant descriptive discourse, the words merely decorate a subject. The last two lines of this sonnet are a summary rather than the emotional resolution of the theme (as they should be).

NOTE:

10a: Probably the best equivalent in English of the Italian sonnet as a form (*sonnet,* original French meaning, equals to ring, to peal, as bells, that is, a short tune).

10b: The sonnet as an English adaptation of the Italian form beginning to degenerate into a short discursive verse form dealing with moral subjects.

The Sonnet Form is *not* a matter of 14 lines, set rhyme scheme, 10 syllables to a line, alternating ascending accents, as the rhetoric books have it. *Sonnet* literally implies the form of the short tune, to which certain Italian poets — Dante, Cavalcanti, and others — wrote words; the form involved the statement of a subject, its development, and resolution. Dissociated from music, the *sonnet* became merely the poor versification of amateurs, without emotion or sense of the relation of the parts of a composition to the whole.

11a_____

As ye came from the holy land
    Of Walsinghame,
Met you not with my true love
    By the way as you came?

How should I know your true love,
    That have met many a one
As I came from the holy land,
    That have come, that have gone?

She is neither white nor brown,
    But as the heavens fair;
There is none hath her form divine
    In the earth or the air.

Such a one did I meet, good sir,
    Such an angelic face
Who like a nymph, like a queen, did appear
    In her gait, in her grace.

She hath left me here alone
    All alone, as unknown,
Who sometime did me lead with herself,
    And me loved as her own.

What 's the cause that she leaves you alone
    And a new way doth take,
That sometime did love you as her own,
    And her joy did you make?

I have loved her all my youth,
    But now am old, as you see:
Love likes not the falling fruit,
    Nor the withered tree.

Know that Love is a careless child,
    And forgets promise past:
He is blind, he is deaf when he list,
    And in faith never fast.

His desire is a dureless content,
    And a trustless joy;
He is won with a world of despair
    And is lost with a toy.

Of womenkind such indeed is the love,
    Or the word love abusèd,
Under which many childish desires
    And conceits are excusèd.

But true love is a durable fire,
    In the mind ever burning,
Never sick, never dead, never cold,
    From itself never turning.

                Anonymous
                16th century

11b

In somer when the shawes (1) be sheyne, (2)
    And leves be large and long,
Hit is full merry in feyre foreste
    To here the foulys (3) song.

To se the dere (4) draw to the dale
    And leve the hilles hee,
And shadow him in the leves grene
    Under the green-wode tree.

Hit befell on Whitsontide
    Early in a May mornyng,
The Sonne up faire can shyne,
    And the briddes merry can syng.

'This is a merry mornyng,' said Litulle Johne,
    'Be Hym that dyd on tre;
A more merry man than I am one
    Lyves not in Christiante.

    (1) woods   (2) bright   (3) birds   (4) deer

'Pluck up thi hert, my dere mayster,'
    Litulle Johne can say,
'And thynk hit is a fulle fayre tyme
    In a mornynge of May.'

Anonymous
16th century

COMMENT:

Two ballads: Preference for one or the other would depend
on sentiment, caring to read at the moment, etc., (granted one
knows that 11b is probably an introduction to a longer ballad
or series of ballads, whereas 11a is complete in itself). Both
examples are quite perfect. The anonymous poet in each case
gives his authoritative version of folk art: specifically, of the
story which has been sung on various occasions by the people,
for many years.

NOTE:

Folk art occurs with inevitable order as part of the growing
history of a people. Its technique is the result of their lives,
their enterprises. There is no use in modern sophistication *trying
to get back* to folk art; the result will always be modern sophistication.

This age, aware of certain processes the sixteenth century
could not possibly be aware of, demands another order (perhaps
disorder) of art:

St. Louis woman with her diamond ring
Leads her man round by her apron string.

But the *essential* technique of folk art (*not* the technique of
rhyme scheme, four line stanzas, etc.) — its simplicity, its whole-
ness of emotional presentation — *can* serve as a guide to any
detail of technique growing out of the living processes of any
age.

12a_____

I have no way and therefore want no eyes;
I stumbled when I saw: full oft 'tis seen,
Our means secure us, and our mere defects
Prove our commodities.

William Shakespeare
King Lear, IV, i
1608

12b_____

Since light so necessary is to life,
And almost life itself, if it be true
That light is in the soul,
She all in every part, why was the sight
To such a tender ball as th' eye confined,
So obvious and so easy to be quencht,
And not, as feeling, through all parts diffused,
That she might look at will through every pore?
Then had I not been thus exiled from light,
As in the land of darkness, yet in light
To live a life half dead, a living death,
And buried; but, O yet more miserable!
Myself my sepulchre, a moving grave;
Buried, yet not exempt,
By privilege of death and burial,
From worst of other evils, pains, and wrongs,
But made hereby obnoxious more
To all the miseries of life,
Life in captivity
Among inhuman foes.

John Milton
Samson Agonistes
1667 - 1671

COMMENT:

Two soliloquies in character: Shakespeare's Gloucester and
Milton's Samson — their unpent reactions to their blindness.

It is the hardest task for even great poets to limit the number of words used to maximum advantage. That is, great poetry achieves a continual growth of meaning (*total poetic emotion*), rather than a maximum of one emotional statement ultimately dissipated by wordiness (two to six ways of saying the same thing over again).

In 12a the poet simply can't leave words alone, "it is such fun" when their same meanings appear in surface-changing, mystifying guises: *Our means secure us* equals *our mere defects prove our commodities,* which says conceptually, but not emotionally, *I . . . want no eyes; I stumbled when I saw.* The last is great poetry, what follows is rhetoric.

In 12b the poet happens to be infatuated with sound, thunder, and fury, and is "building" a verse paragraph. After line 9 (and lines 4 to 9 are great poetry), Milton adds nothing to the emotional intensity of the passage.

NOTE:

The lines of poetry of great emotional significance in any age are rare. To attain, therefore, an accurate criticism of them and of the lesser work which surrounds them, reading should not shun analysis.

13a_____

How should I your true love know
    From another one?
By his cockle hat and staff
    And his sandal shoon.

He is dead and gone, lady,
    He is dead and gone;
At his head a grass green turf,
    At his heels a stone.

White his shroud as the mountain snow —
    Larded with sweet flowers;
Which bewept to the grave did go
    With true-love showers.

        William Shakespeare
        Hamlet, IV, v
        1603

13b_____

Hark! now everything is still,
The screech-owl and the whistler shrill
Call upon our dame aloud,
And bid her quickly don her shroud.
Much you had of land and rent:
Your length in clay 's now competent.
A long war disturbed your mind:
Here your perfect peace is signed.
Of what is 't fools make such vain keeping?
Sin their conception, their birth weeping,
Their life a general mist of error,
Their death a hideous storm of terror.
Strew your hair with powders sweet,
Don clean linen, bathe your feet,
And — the foul fiend more to check
A crucifix let bless your neck.

'Tis now full tide 'tween night and day;
End your groan and come away.

> John Webster
> *The Duchess of Malfi*, IV, ii
> 1616

COMMENT:

13a: A song that will sing to a tune. 13b: A "song" —
that is, a *lyric* — that will not sing to music, but must be de-
claimed or intoned. 13a achieves the effect of terror in the
melody of the words. 13b achieves the effect of terror in the
extravagant cumulativeness of its tolling sounds and melo-
dramatic imagery.

NOTE:

Except for lines 5 to 7, 13b does not seem so inevitable and
necessary a poetic achievement as 13a. In poetry, the melo-
dramatic, though it may achieve an "atmosphere," often falls
short of the essential.

14a_____

Let me not to the marriage of true minds
Admit impediments. Love is not love
Which alters when it alteration finds,
Or bends with the remover to remove:
O, no! it is an ever-fixed mark,
That looks on tempests and is never shaken;
It is the star to every wandering bark,
Whose worth's unknown, although his height be taken.
Love's not Time's fool, though rosy lips and cheeks
Within his bending sickle's compass come;
Love alters not with his brief hours and weeks,
But bears it out even to the edge of doom.
　　　If this be error and upon me proved
　　　I never writ, nor no man ever loved.
　　　　　　　　　　　William Shakespeare
　　　　　　　　　　　Sonnet 116
　　　　　　　　　　　1608-9

14b_____

Things base and vile, holding no quantity,
Love can transpose to form and dignity.
Love looks not with the eyes but with the mind,
And therefore is wing'd Cupid painted blind.
Nor hath Love's mind of any judgement taste;
Wings and no eyes figure unheedy haste;
And therefore is Love said to be a child,
Because in choice he is so oft beguil'd.
　　　　　　　　　　　William Shakespeare
　　　　　　　　　　　A Midsummer-Night's Dream, I, i
　　　　　　　　　　　1594-5

COMMENT:

14a: Shakespeare telling the laity of love. Lines 1 to 4
command the intelligence as well as the cadence. The rest of
the sonnet is rhetoric (ornamental as against definitive speech):
striking metaphor, as in lines 9 and 10, suggesting almost any-

thing and everything in connection with a particular blend of images; but nevertheless arbitrary, inasmuch as what is suggested is very rich but never too definite.

14b: The intelligence — in these lines, the awareness of a continuous, unbroken line of melody carrying the succinct meaning of words — defines love with the methods of positive and deductive science. The emotion is not less for following an organic exactness of speech, rather than a series of poetic allusions or profuseness of sentiment.

NOTE:

Shakespeare probably never read Cavalcanti's *Donna mi prega,* but lines 1 to 4 of *Sonnet* 116 and 14b have the substance of Cavalcanti. (European literary tradition of 1290 to 1609.)

15a_____

I struck the board, and cried, no more;
    I will abroad.
What! Shall I ever sigh and pine?
My lines and life are free; free as the road,
Loose as the wind, as large as store;
    Shall I be still in suit? . . .
        Away; take heed
        I will abroad.
Call in thy death's-head there: tie up thy fears.
    He that forbears
    To suit and serve his need,
    Deserves his load.
But as I raved and grew more fierce and wild
        At every word
Methought I heard one calling, *Child*:
    And I replied, *My Lord.*

George Herbert (1593-1632)
The Collar

15b_____

My starveling bull
Ah! woe is me!
In pasture full
How lean is he!

Thomas Fuller
The Holy State
1641

COMMENT:

Examples of religious verse of the 17th century. 15a: One of George Herbert's best devotional lyrics. 15b: Keen, religious satire.

NOTE:

Recent critics of literature have expressed the opinion that the beliefs implied or held in a poem influence the reader's appreciation. The opposite opinion would be that a poem is an emotional object defined not by the beliefs it deals with, but by its *technique* and the *poetic conviction or mastery* with which these beliefs are expressed.

16a————

Welcome, maids of honour,
    You do bring
    In the Spring
And wait upon her.

She has virgins many,
    Fresh and fair;
    Yet you are
More sweet than any.

You're the maiden posies
    And so graced
    To be placed
'Fore damask roses.

Yet, though thus respected
    By-and-by
    Ye do die,
Poor girls, neglected.

Robert Herrick
Violets
c. 1648

16b————

Is this a fast, to keep
    The larder lean,
    And clean
From fat of veals and sheep?

Is it to quit the dish
    Of flesh, yet still
    To fill
The platter high with fish?

Is it to fast an hour
    Or ragged to go,
    Or show
A downcast look, and sour?

No; 'tis a fast, to dole
  Thy sheaf of wheat
    And meat
Unto the hungry soul.

It is to fast from strife,
  From old debate
    And hate;
To circumcise thy life;

To show a heart grief-rent;
  To starve thy sin,
    Not bin.
And that 's to keep thy Lent.

> Robert Herrick
> *To Keep A True Lent*
> 1648

COMMENT:

The words and cadences of 16a are written for music. None of the words edge out of the melody. Even heavy words like *respected* and *neglected* are resolved lightly.

The words of 16b are charged with more involved matter than the clear image of flowers regretted in song. The poetic emotion of 16b is spoken righteous indignation. The type of word recurring often in 16b is the sharp image, staccato, one syllable, rhymed for emphasis. The rhymes, without interfering with the movement of impassioned speech, never smooth over the cadence so that it will sing to music as in 16a. Herrick did not intend 16b to be sung. On the other hand, Herrick did not need to lengthen the lines of 16b to obtain his effect of resonant, impassioned diction. He merely gave the single words of 16b more volume than those of 16a.

NOTE:

There probably is no such absolute dictum as the "non-poetic" word; any word may be poetic if used in the right order, with the right cadence, with a definite aim in view: whether it be music (i.e. lyricism) of statement; suggestion of an accompanying tune; image; relation of concepts or ideas; or a context which is all of these things at once. Thus it would be ridiculous to say Herrick's words, *larder, fat, veals, platter,* as used in their context, are "non-poetic."

Condensation is more than half of compositon. The rest is proper breathing space, ease, grace.

17a_____

The mighty Mother, and her Son, who brings
The Smithfield Muses to the ear of Kings,
I sing. Say ye, her instruments, the great,
Called to this Work by Dulness, Jove, and Fate;
You by whose care, in vain decry'd, and curst,
Still Dunce the second reigns like Dunce the first;
Say, how the Goddess bade Britania sleep,
And pour'd her spirit o'er the land and deep.

> Alexander Pope
> *Dunciad*
> 1728

17b_____

The mighty Spirit and its power which stains
The bloodless cheek, and vivifies the brains,
I sing. Say ye, its fiery Vot'ries true,
The jovial Curate, and the shrill-tongu'd Shrew;
Ye, in the floods of limpid poison nurst,
Where Bowl the second charms like Bowl the first;
Say, how and why the sparkling ill is shed,
The Heart which hardens, and which rules the Head.

> George Crabbe
> *Inebriety* I
> 1775

17c_____

"Dispatch," says she, "the business you pretend,
Your beastly visit to your drunken friend,
A bottle ever makes you look so fine;
Methinks I long to smell you stink of wine.
Your country drinking breath 's enough to kill;
Sour ale corrected with a lemon-peel. . . . "

> Earl of Rochester
> *A Letter from Artemisa in the Town,
> To Chloe in the Country*
> c. 1670

17d_____

In Easter-term she gets her a new gown,
When my young master's worship comes to town,
From pedagogue and mother just set free,
The heir and hopes of a great family;
Who with strong beer and beef the country rules,
And ever since the Conquest have been fools;
And now, with careful prospect to maintain
This character, lest crossing of the strain
Should mend the booby breed, his friends provide
A cousin of his own to be his bride.

> Earl of Rochester
> *A Letter from Artemisa in the Town,*
> *To Chloe in the Country*
> c. 1670

17e_____

Footsteps shuffled on the stair,
Under the firelight, under the brush, her hair
Spread out in fiery points
Glowed into words, then would be savagely still.

"My nerves are bad to-night. Yes, bad. Stay with me.
Speak to me. Why do you never speak? Speak.
What are you thinking of? What thinking? What?
I never know what you are thinking. Think."

> T. S. Eliot
> *The Waste Land*
> 1922

COMMENT:

Examples of satirical verse.

17a: The heroic nature of the burlesque combined with the indefinitenes of the words makes the satire too heavy, and the verse too light, so that both lose point. *Britania's sleep,* a nation's *Dulness,* etc. can be described definitely as social and historical scene. 17a does not do this (though there is wit —

brilliant presentation of relation — in the line *Still Dunce the second reigns like Dunce the first.*)

17b: An imitation of 17a; the verse form applied to a different subject. All the faults of 17a are copied. The best line, *Where Bowl the second charms like Bowl the first,* is modelled after Pope's best line in 17a.

17c does definitely what 17b fails to do. 17d does definitely what 17a fails to do. In 17e the satire is *implicit* and thus not only more pointed, but more touching. The poetic-dramatic situation is presented *without any comment.*

NOTE:

Writing presents the finished matter, *it does not comment.* Satiric verse, at its best, does not exist in a vacuum of abstractions. If the subject dealt with is a drunk, it is better to *render the person* than to talk about *inebriety.* If the subject is the decay of a certain social order, it is better to give specific examples of that decay than to treat of it *generally.* A poet's dramatic sense is often a short cut to effective implication *as well as* to effective presentation.

Poetry is information: the effectiveness of the cadence of a line is usually in direct proportion to the definitness of the words used in that line. Cadence plus definite language equal the full meaning.

18a_____

    "Homer! nay, Pope! (for never will I seek
Applause for learning — nought have I with Greek —)
Gives us the secrets of his pagan hell,
Where ghost with ghost in sad communion dwell;
Where shade meets shade, and round the gloomy meads
They glide and speak of old heroic deeds —
What fields they conquered, and what foes they slew
And sent to join the melancholy crew.
    When a new spirit in that world was found,
A thousand shadowy forms came flitting round;
Those who had known him, fond inquiries made:—
'Of all we left, inform us, gentle shade,
'Now as we lead thee in our realms to dwell,
'Our twilight groves, and meads of asphodel.'
    What paints the poet, is our station here,
Where we like ghosts and flitting shades appear:
This is the hell he sings, and here we meet,
And former deeds to new-made friends repeat;
Heroic deeds, which here obtain us fame,
And are in fact the causes why we came.
Yes! this dim region is old Homer's hell,
Abate but groves and meads of asphodel.
    Here, when a stranger from your world we spy,
We gather round him and for news apply;
He hears unheeding, nor can speech endure,
But shivering gazes on the vast obscure.
We, smiling, pity, and by kindness show
We felt his feelings and his terrors know;
Then speak of comfort — time will give him sight
Where now 'tis dark; where now 'tis wo, delight.

George Crabbe
The Borough
Prisons, Letter **XXIII**
1810

18b_____

O terror! what hath she perceived? — O joy!
What doth she look on? — whom doth she behold?
Her Hero slain upon the beach of Troy?
His vital presence? his corporeal mould?
It is — if sense deceive her not — 'tis He!
And a god leads him, wingèd Mercury!

Mild Hermes spake — and touched her with his wand
That calms all fear; "Such grace hath crowned thy prayer,
Laodamia! that at Jove's command
Thy Husband walks the path of upper air:
He comes to tarry with thee three hours' space;
Accept the gift, behold him face to face!"

Forth sprang the impassioned Queen her Lord to clasp;
Again that consummation she essayed;
But unsubstantial. Form eludes her grasp
As often as that eager grasp was made.
The Phantom parts — but parts to re-unite,
And re-assume his place before her sight.

"Protesiláus, lo! thy guide is gone!
Confirm, I pray, the vision with thy voice:
This is our palace — yonder is thy throne;
Speak, and the floor thou tread'st on will rejoice.
Not to appal me have the gods bestowed
This precious boon; and blest a sad abode."

William Wordsworth
Laodamia
1814

COMMENT:

Readable, honest attempts at good writing, these can hardly
be said to have the emotional effectiveness of great poetry. "And
certainly were it the principal employment of a man's life to
compose verses, it might seem reasonable to expect that he would
continue to improve as long as he continued to live;" (George

Crabbe, *Preface to Poems,* ed. of 1807). It might seem reasonable to expect the same of the life of a poem.

NOTE:

The "classics" usually *date* when their matter resembles good period furniture, museum pieces and antiques. Elegance and correct versification meant for declamation are not enough to compel permanent interest, as poetry. As poetry, only objectified emotion endures. 18a and 18b are readable for the narrative, the ease of the verse technique casting things seen on the visual imagination, the drama, and an occasional line of objectified emotional intensity that seems to carry over into the ineffective lines.

19a_____

Ae night the storm the steeples rocked,
Poor Labour sweet in sleep was locked,
While burns, wi' snawy wreaths up-choked,
                                        Wild-eddying swirl,
Or, thro' the mining outlet bocked,
                            Down headlong hurl;
                                    Robert Burns
                                    A Winter Night
                                    1786

19b_____

Blow, blow, ye winds, with heavier gust!
And freeze, thou bitter-biting frost!
Descend, ye chilly smothering snows!
Not all your rage, as now united, shows
        More hard unkindness unrelenting,
        Vengeful malice, unrepenting,
Than heav'n-illumin'd man on brother man bestows!
        See stern Oppression's iron grip,
            Or mad Ambition's gory hand,
        Sending, like blood-hounds from the slip;
            Woe, want, and murder o'er a land!
                                    Robert Burns
                                    A Winter Night
                                    1786

19c_____

Ye see yon birkie, ca'd a lord,
        Wha struts, and stares, and a' that;
Tho' hundreds worship at his word,
        He's but a coof for a' that:
            For a' that, and a' that,
                His riband, star, and a' that;
            The man of independent mind,
                He looks and laughs at a' that.

Then let us pray that come it may,
    As come it will for a' that;
That sense and worth, o'er a' the earth,
    May bear the gree, and a' that.
        For a' that, and a' that,
           It's coming yet, for a' that,
      That man to man the warld o'er
        Shall brothers be for a' that.

                 Robert Burns
                 For A' That and A' That
                 1794

COMMENT:

19a: Presents accurately an image connected with the wintry environment of *Labour*. Line 2, with the exception of the word *Poor* would seem to lack conviction. In any case, the emotion seems to derive from Burns' literary reading, rather than from his mastery of the subject matter.

19b: Evidently derivative (with an eye on Shakespeare — his declamatory rhetoric). Burns imitates the "grand manner," "the air of the classical," but the result is affected, without assured factual basis, without the comprehension, general as well as tehcnical, which makes a work a classic.

19c: The poet's facts and his expression of them have been fused into a true classic recognizable as Burns at his best.

NOTE:

Good poetry is the barest — most essentially complete — form of presenting a subject; good poetry does not linger to embroider words around a subject. A gift of description, as in 19a, may be far from great poetry, but it will do to present an image or a situation. Bombast and pseudo-heroic generalities (19b, lines 8 and 9) evade definite information. Good poetry is definite information on the subject dealt with, on the movement of the lines of verse, and on the emotion of verbal construction. Satire and humor, as in 19c, serve as basic impulse for song and poetic insight (technique and comprehension). Burns' use of *a' that* and *for a' that* is not monotonous, but varied.

20a————

I arise from dreams of thee
In the first sweet sleep of night,
When the winds are breathing low,
And the stars are shining bright:
I arise from dreams of thee
And a spirit in my feet
Hath led me — who knows how!
To thy chamber window, Sweet!

The wandering airs they faint
On the dark, the silent stream —
And the Champak odours fail
Like sweet thoughts in a dream;
The nightingale's complaint,
It dies upon her heart; —
As I must die on thine.
O! belovèd as thou art.

P. B. Shelley
An Indian Serenade
1819

20b————

I awoke in the Midsummer not to call night, in the white and
the walk of the morning
The moon, dwindled and thinned to the fringe of a fingernail
held to the candle,
Or paring of paradisaical fruit, lovely in waning but lustreless,
Stepped from the stool, drew back from the barrow, of dark
Maenefa the mountain;
A cusp still clasped him, a fluke yet fanged him, entangled him,
not quit utterly.
This was the prized, the desirable sight, unsought, presented
so easily,
Parted me leaf and leaf, divided me, eyelid and eyelid of
slumber.

Gerard Manley Hopkins
Moonrise
1876

COMMENT:

20a: The cadence when its emotional integrity is tenuous, becomes too facile. The words are too often carried along in a *lull* of sound (of no intrinsic value) till they lose their connotative meanings. Or, the lines become banal.

20b: The cadence, its emotional integrity, tends to be so carefully true, worked out, measured, that the attention is forced to stop and define almost every word. The connotations of the words are never passed over, but they are often so rich in suggestion (many shades of meanings packed into one word) that the result is an ambiguity of meanings giving the effect of vagueness (as, *divided me, eyelid and eyelid of slumber.*)

NOTE:

It is not enough, critically, to say that 20b is better than 20a. In these two examples, the faults are not so obviously glaring, and the qualities not so readily evident, to permit too easy generalization. The criticism of 20a and 20b would be better supported by detailed analysis.

20a: *I arise from dreams of thee* — the ease and inevitability of the spoken emotion resolved into musical content, but the order of the vowel sounds is perhaps too monotonous to be sung; the next line continues on the same level of attainment, but begins to lose intensity in *of night;* line 3, "poetically" affected, is a continued falling off; *winds breathing low* shows lack of restraint, the musical effect is too patent; line 4 is obviously nothing but a filler in the stanzaic structure.

20b: Line 1, *I awoke . . . not to call night* is awkward syntactically, ambiguous; the concluding half of this line is a good image, but the verse drags, becomes repetitious in the phrases — *in the white, and the walk of the morning.* The next line is a masterful example of the visual imagination forming a relation of images, of facts, hitherto unrelated, so that the result is a new experience. *A cusp still clasped him* — the effect is in the stress of repeated sounds. Next line — *This was the prized . . . ,* the cadence of the verse and the cadence of the spoken meaning harmonize perfectly.

Since the qualities, "not so readily evident," of 20a and 20b would exist in the proper proportion in better writing, it is advisable to notice these qualities, but not to use either 20a or 20b entire as models for judgment. 20a and 20b are *special cases* for a "laboratory analysis" of poetry, and *not revealing examples* of good style, of a perfect order of emotion, leading to general, basic decisions on the materials and nature of poetic writing.

21a_____

These wretched Comparini were once gay
And galliard, of the modest middle class:
Born in this quarter seventy years ago
And married young, they lived the accustomed life,
Citizens as they were of good repute:
And, childless, naturally took their ease
With only their two selves to care about
And use the wealth for: wealthy is the word,
Since Pietro was possessed of house and land —
And specially one house, when good days smiled,
In Via Vittoria, the aspectable street
Where he lived mainly; but another house
Of less pretension did he buy betimes,
The villa, meant for jaunts and jollity,
I' the Pauline district, to be private there —
Just what puts murder in an enemy's head.
Moreover — here's the worm i' the core, the germ
O' the rottenness and ruin which arrived, —
He owned some usufruct, had moneys' use
Lifelong, but to determine with his life
In heirs' default: so, Pietro craved an heir, —

Robert Browning
The Ring and The Book II
1868-9

21b_____

Weep Venus and ye
Adorable Three
Who Venus for ever environ.
Pounds, shillings and pence
And shrewd sober sense
Have clapt the straight waistcoat on***

Off Lainot and Turk
With pistol and dirk,
Nor palace nor pinnace set fire on,

The cord's fatal jerk
Has done its last work
And the noose is now slipped upon***

Walter Savage Landor
Epithalamium
c. 1846

COMMENT:

Two poetic records of social strata — society in Italy in the
17th century, society in England in the 19th century. In 21a
implicit satire finds its form as narrative poetry. In 21b satire
is formally conveyed by the polished cantabile quality of the verse.

NOTE:

The emotional quality of good poetry is founded on exact
observation which is often a combination of humor *plus* sense.

22a_____

Is she wronged? — To the rescue of her honour,
   My heart!
Is she poor? — What costs it to be styled a donor?
   Merely an earth to cleave, a sea to part.
But that fortune should have thrust all this upon her!
   ('Nay, list!' — bade Kate the queen;
And still cried the maiden, binding her tresses,
   ' 'Tis only a page that carols unseen,
'Fitting your hawks their jesses!')

> Robert Browning
> *Pippa Passes*
> 1841

22b_____

Where shall we find her, how shall we sing to her,
   Fold our hands round her knees, and cling?
O that man's heart were as fire and could spring to her,
   Fire, or the strength of the streams that spring!
For the stars and the winds are unto her
As raiment, as songs of the harp-player;
For the risen stars and the fallen cling to her,
   And the southwest-wind and the west-wind sing.

> A. C. Swinburne
> Chorus from *Atalanta*
> 1865

COMMENT:

22a: A stanza obviously to be set to music, but also an exact statement. The dramatic detail is developed precisely in the melody of the words.

22b: A blend of too expansive rhythms and interjections. The sound of the lines tends to reiterate, but does not find melodic form. This example is interesting metrical experiment (imitative of the Greek chorus, etc.). It has emotional drive. The chief trouble with such verse is, it doesn't seem to matter what it says. In particular it was intended to mean the *Coming of Spring*. It might mean that and almost anything else. Perhaps the most definite meaning to be obtained from it is the feeling of a very grandiose shadow built upon very little. More precisely:

> *For the stars and the winds are unto her*
> *As raiment, as songs of the harp-player,*

— evidently a puzzling proportion — four things are equated to one thing (*her*) ; *but the four things* (*stars, winds, raiment, songs of the harp-player*) are not equated to each other.

NOTE:

There is verse movement which directs matter and sense and implied musical accompaniment to a fitting end: A. There is verse movement which rolls in one place so that sense, matter, etc. seem to have no beginning or end: B. A is prferable to B. The idea of an equation touched upon in the comment does not mean that the laws of mathematics are applicable to an analysis of poetry. The poet's actual writing down of his poem may be pretty much, or very much an unconscious (as opposed to a logical) process. But when the words of a poem, intended to denote certain "happenings" or "things," are jogged about so that only noble vagueness is denoted, the poet has failed in his task of *presentation*.

23a_____

Merry Margaret
    As midsummer flower,
Gentle as falcon
    Or hawk of the tower,
With solace and gladness,
Much mirth and no madness;
All good and no badness,
So joyously,
So maidenly,
So womanly,
Her demeaning
In every thing
Far far passing
That I can endite
Or suffice to write
Of merry Margaret,
    As midsummer flower,
Gentle as falcon
    Or hawk of the tower.

As patient and as still,
And as full of good will,
As fair Isaphill,
Coliander,
Sweet pomander,
Good Cassander,
Steadfast of thought,
Well made, well wrought.
Far may be sought
Erst that ye can find
So courteous, so kind,
As merry Margaret,
    This midsummer flower,
Gentle as falcon
    Or hawk of the tower.

John Skelton
To Mistress Margaret Hussey
16th century

23b___

Lalage's coming:
Where is she now, O?
Turning to bow, O,
And smile, is she,
Just at parting,
Parting, parting,
As she is starting
To come to me?

Where is she now, O,
Now, and now, O,
Shadowing a bough, O,
Of hedge or tree
As she is rushing,
Rushing, rushing,
Gossamers brushing
To come to me?

Lalage's coming;
Where is she now, O;
Climbing the brow, O,
Of hills I see?
Yes, she is nearing,
Nearing, nearing,
Weather unfearing
To come to me.

Near is she now, O,
Now, and now, O;
Milk the rich cow, O,
Forward the tea;
Shake the down bed for her,
Linen sheets spread for her,
Drape round the head for her
Coming to me.

Lalage's coming,
She's nearer now, O,

End anyhow, O,
To-day's husbandry!
Would a gilt chair were mine,
Slippers of vair were mine,
Brushes for hair were mine
Of ivory!

> Thomas Hardy
> *Moments of Vision*
> Timing Her (Written to an old folk-tune)
> c. 1916

COMMENT:

Probably intended for dance tunes or written with dance tunes in mind. 23a: The periodic recurrence of the first four lines suggests a round (dance). 23b: In the beat of certain repeated words, such as *rushing, rushing* is the cadence of a jig. The musical form of 23a does not hinder the presentation; the music of 23b does, by becoming repetitious.

NOTE:

Poetry does not arise and exist in a vacuum. It is one of the arts — sometimes individual, sometimes collective in origin — and reflects economic and social status of peoples; their language habits arising out of everyday matter of fact; the constructions which the intelligence and the emotions make over and apart from the everyday after it has been understood and generally experienced.

Certain aspects of construction and design are common to all the arts: 23a and 23b carry over from folk dance and folk music, the recurrence of rhythms, the strong cadence, the heavy beat of reiteration, the folk quality of emphasizing a thing over and over again — with the body, with the hands, with the feet, with the voice — so as to make certain that the sincerity of an emotion concerning one's existence has been conveyed.

The less poetry is concerned with the everyday existence and the rhythmic talents of a people, the less *readable* that poetry is likely to be. But the forms of particular communication — which are necessary enough for a varied life — may never, in any society, be absorbed as automatically as air.

24a_____

I have a gentil cok
        Croweth me day;
He doth me risen erly
        My matines for to say.

I have a gentil cok;
        Comen (1) he is of grete; (2)
His comb is of red corel,
        His tail is of get. (3)

I have a gentil cok;
        Comen he is of kinde;
His comb is of red corel,
        His tail is of inde. (4)

His legges ben of asour, (5)
        So gentil and so smale;
His sporès (6) arn of silver white
        Into the wortèwale. (7)

His eynen arn of cristal,
        Loken (8) all in aumber; (9)
And every night he percheth him
        In mine ladyes chaumber.

                                    Anonymous
                                    15th century

(1) descended   (2) great (stock, lineage)   (3) jet   (4) indigo
    (5) azure   (6) spurs   (7) the skin of the claws
            (8) set (literally locked)   (9) amber

24b_____

so much depends
upon

a red wheel
barrow

glazed with rain
water

beside the white
chickens.

William Carlos Williams
Spring and All
1923

COMMENT:

24a: This is material for mosaic work, or stained glass, though it has been treated in words. 24b: But for the first four words, this description might have been painted.

Whatever the symbolic implication of 24a, if any, the attention of the poet seems to be taken up by sheer play; by the opulence of lovely, but artificial conditions. The white chickens of 24b are even more gentle than the mosaic *cok* (24a) descended of gentility. The more than visual importance of the simple rural objects observed is only too evident in the short thoughtful cadences of this poem.

NOTE:

It may take only four words to shift the level at which emotion is held from neatness of surface to comprehension which includes surface and what is under it.

25a＿＿＿＿＿

De darkeys got so lonesome libb'n
    In de log hut on de lawn,
Dey moved dere tings into massa's parlor
    For to keep it while he gone.
Dar's wine an' cider in de kitchin,
    An' de darkeys dey hab some,
I spec it will be all fiscated,
    When de Lincum sojers come.
        De massa run, ha, ha!
        De darkey stay, ho, ho!
        It mus' be now de kingdum comin',
        An' de yar ob jubilo.
                H. C. Work
                The Year of Jubilee
                (Sung by the negro troops
                as they entered Richmond)
                1865

25b＿＿＿＿＿

Bestis [1] and thos foules [2]
    The fisses in the flode,
And euch schef [3] alives
    Makid of bone and blode,
Whan he commith to the world
    He doth ham silf [4] sum gode,
Al bot the wrech brol [5]
    That is of Adamis blode.
        Lollai, lollai, litil child!
            To kar [6] ertow [7] bemette;
        Thou nost noght this worldis wild
            Bifor the is isette.
                Anglo-Irish dialect
                c. 1308 - 1318
                (written apparently in
                Gray Abbey, a Franciscan house,
                in Kildare.)

[1] beasts   [2] birds   [3] creature   [4] himself
    [5] child   [6] care   [7] art thou

COMMENT:

25a: A satirical marching song. 25b: A lullaby; a lament; anonymous. Each example is a record of things seen, ideas felt, emotions gone through, and sung.

NOTE:

25a and 25b depend upon the sincere convictions and the almost unexplainable completeness of the art of simplicity out of which all folk poetry is made. Such poetry is not the property of the few "arty," but of everybody.

PART III

FURTHER COMPARISONS

"I will conclude by adducing a further argument founded upon the, to me, unphilosophical nature of the force to which the phenomena are . . . referred."

MICHAEL FARADAY

1a_____

The first that press'd in was Elpenor's soul
His body in the broad-way'd earth as yet
Unmourned, unburied by us, since we swet
With other urgent labours. Yet his smart
I wept to see, and rued it from my heart,
Enquiring how he could before me be
That came by ship? He, mourning, answered me:
'In Circe's house, the spite some spirit did bear,
And the unspeakable good liquor there,
Hath been my bane; for, being to descend
A ladder much in height, I did not tend
My way well down, but forwards made a proof
To tread the rounds, and from the very roof
Fell on my neck, and brake it; and this made
My soul thus visit this infernal shade.

1b_____

But not for mind or foot was that way made.
Death is not knowing what is not a shadow.
And nothing is. That now is what he says.

1c_____

Night swallowed the sun as
the fish swallowed Jonas.

1d_____

And the woman said unto Saul,
I saw gods ascending out of the earth.
And he said unto her,
What form is he of?
And she said, An old man cometh up;
and he is covered with a mantle.

2a _____

Delight of humankind, and gods above
Parent of Rome, propitious Queen of Love!
Whose vital power, air, earth, and sea supplies,
And breeds whate'er is born beneath the rolling skies;
For every kind, by thy prolific might,
Springs, and beholds the regions of the light.
Thee, goddess, thee the clouds and tempests fear,
And at thy pleasing presence disappear;
For thee the land in fragrant flowers is drest;
For thee the ocean smiles, and smoothes her wavy breast,
And heaven itself with more serene and purer light is blest . . .
Through all the living regions dost thou move,
And scatterest, where thou goest, the kindly seeds of love.
Since, then, the race of every living thing
Obeys thy power; since nothing new can spring
Without thy warmth, without thy influence bear,
Or beautiful or lovesome can appear;
Be thou my aid, my tuneful song inspire,
And kindle with thy own productive fire;

2b _____

Darling of Gods and men, beneath the sliding stars
You fill rich earth and buoyant sea with your presence
For every living thing achieves its life through you,
Rises and sees the sun. For you the sky is clear
The tempests still. Deft earth scatters her gentle flowers
The level ocean laughs, the softened heavens glow
With generous light for you. In the first days of spring
When the untrammelled allrenewing southwind blows
The birds exult in you and herald your coming.
Then the shy cattle leap and swim the brooks for love.
Everywhere, through all seas mountains and waterfalls,
Love caresses all hearts and kindles all creatures
To overmastering lust and ordained renewals.
Therefore, since you alone control the sum of things

And nothing without you comes forth into the light
And nothing beautiful or glorious can be
Without you, Alma Venus! trim my poetry
With your grace; and give peace to write and read and think.

3a_____

Envy why carpest thou my time is spent so ill,
And termst my works fruits of an idle quill?
Or that unlike the line from whence I come,
Wars dusty honours are refused being young?
Nor that I study not the brawling laws
Nor set my voice to sale in every cause?
Thy scope is mortal, mine eternal fame,
That all the world may ever chant my name.
Homer shall live while *Tenedos* stands and *Ide,*
Or into Sea, swift *Simois* doth slide.
Ascraeus lives, while grapes with new wine swell,
Or men with crooked Sickles corn down fell.
The world shall of *Callimachus* ever speak,
His art excelled, although his wit was weak.
For ever lasts high *Sophocles* proud vaine
With Sun and Moon *Aratus* shall remain.
While bond-men cheat, fathers hard, bawds whorish,
And strumpets flatter, shall *Menander* flourish . . .
Till *Cupid's* Bow and fiery Shafts be broken,
Thy verses sweet *Tibullus* shall be spoken.
And *Gallus* shall be known from East to West,
So shall *Licoris* whom he loved best.

3b_____

Envy, why twitst thou me, my Time's spent ill?
And call'st my verse fruits of an idle quill?
Or that (unlike the line from whence I sprung)
Wars dusty honors I pursue not young?
Or that I studie not, the tedious laws;
And prostitute my voyce in every cause?
Thy scope is mortal; mine eternal Fame,
Which through the world shall ever chant my name.
Homer will live, whilst *Tenedos* stands, and *Ide,*
Or to the sea, fleet *Simais* doth slide:
And so shall *Hesiod* too, while vines do bear,

Or crooked sickles crop the ripened ear,
Callimachus, though in Invention low,
Shall still be sung, since he in Art doth flowe.
No losse shall come to *Sophocles'* proud vein
With Sun and Moon *Aratus* shall remain.
Whilst Slaves be false, Fathers hard and Bawds be whorish,
Whilst Harlots flatter, shall *Menander* flourish . . .
Till *Cupids* fires be out, and his bow broken,
Thy verses (neat *Tibullus*) shall be spoken.
Our *Gallus* shall be known from East to West:
So shall *Licoris*, whom he now loves best.

4a_____

Ye Ayres and windes: ye Elves of Hilles, of Brookes, of Woods
    alone,
Of standing Lakes, and of the Night approach ye every chone.
Through helpe of whom (the crooked bankes much wondring
    at the thing)
I have compelled streams to run cleane back ward' to their spring.
By charmes I make the calme seas rough, and make ye rough
    Seas plaine
And cover all the Skie with Cloudes, and chase them thence
    again.
By charmes I rayse and lay the windes, and burst the Vipers jaw,
And from the bowels of the Earth both stones and trees doe
    drawe.
Whole woods and Forestes I remove: I make the Mountaines
    shake,
And even the earth it selfe to grone and fearfully to quake.
I call up dead men from their graves: and thee O lightsome
    Moone
I darken oft, though beaten brasse abate thy perill soone
Our Sorcerie dimmes the Morning faire, and darkes ye Sun at
    Noone.

4b_____

Ye elves of hills, brooks, standing lakes, and groves;
And ye that on the sands with printless foot
Do chase the ebbing Neptune, and do fly him
When he comes back; you demi-puppets that
By moonshine do the green sour ringlets make,
Whereof the ewe not bites; and you whose pastime
Is to make midnight mushrooms, that rejoice
To hear the solemn curfew; by whose aid —
Weak masters though ye be — I have bedimm'd
The noontide sun, call'd forth the mutinous winds,
And 'twixt the green sea and the azured vault
Set roaring war: to the dread rattling thunder

Have I given fire, and rifted Jove's stout oak
With his own bolt; the strong-based promontory
Have I made shake, and by the spurs pluck'd up
The pine and cedar: graves at my command
Have waked their sleepers, oped, and let 'em forth
By my so potent art.

5a_____

Wandering through many countries and over many
seas I come, my brother, to these sorrowful obsequies,
to present you with the last guerdon of death, and
speak, though in vain, to your silent ashes, since
fortune has taken your own self away from me — alas,
my brother, so cruelly torn from me! Yet now
meanwhile take these offerings, which by the custom
of our fathers have been handed down — a sorrowful
tribute — for a funeral sacrifice; take them, wet with
many tears of a brother, and for ever, O my brother,
hail and farewell!

5b_____

O how shall I warble myself for the dead one there I loved?
And how shall I deck my song for the large sweet soul that
    has gone?
And what shall my perfume be for the grave of him I love?
Sea-winds blown from east and west,
Blown from the Eastern sea and blown from the Western sea,
    till there on the prairies meeting,
These and with these and the breath of my chant,
I'll perfume the grave of him I love.

5c_____

(ponder,darling,these busted statues
of yon motheaten forum be aware
notice what hath remained
— the stone cringes
clinging to the stone,how obsolete

lips utter their extant smile . . . .

6a_____

Before his regale hie magnificens
Mysty vapour upspryngand, sweit as sens, (1)
In smoky soppys (2) of donk (3) dewis wak (4)
Moich (5) hailsum stovys (6) ourheldand (7) the slak; (8)
The aureat (9) fanys of hys trone soverane
With glytrand glans ourspred the occiane (10)
The large fludis lemand (11) all of lycht
Bot with a blenk of his supernale sycht.
Forto behald it was a glore (12) to se
The stabbit (13) wyndis and the cawmyt (14) see, (15)
The soft sesson, the firmament sereyn,
The lowne (16) illumynat ayr, and fyrth (17) ameyn; (18)
The sylver-scalyt fyschis on the greit (19)
Ourthwort cleir stemys sprynkland (20) for the heyt,
With fynnys schynand broun as synopar, (21)
And chyssell talys, stowrand heir and thar;
The new cullour alychtnyng all the landis
Forgane (22) thir stannyris (23) schane the beriall (24) strandis,
Quhil the reflex of the diurnal bemys
The beyn (25) bonkis (26) kest ful of variant glemys.

(1) incense   (2) juices   (3) dank   (4) moist   (5) moist; misty
(6) vapours   (7) covering over   (8) hollows, dales   (9) golden
(10) ocean   (11) glittering   (12) glory   (13) quieted   (14) calmed
(15) sea   (16) still   (17) frith, bay   (18) mild   (19) gravel
(20) moving swiftly with undulatory motion   (21) cinnabar   (22) against
(23) stones   (24) beryl-like   (25) pleasant   (26) banks

6b_____

Forthwith the Sounds and Seas, each Creek and Bay
With Frie innumerable swarme, and Shoales
Of Fish that with thir Finns and shining Scales
Glide under the green Wave, in Sculles that oft
Bank the mid Sea: part single or with mate
Graze the Sea weed thir pasture, and through Groves
Of Coral stray, or sporting with quick glance
Show to the Sun thir wav'd coats dropt with Gold,
Or in their Pearlie shells at ease, attend

Moist nutriment, or under Rocks thir food
In jointed Armour watch: on smoothe the Seale,
And bended Dolphins play: part huge of bulk
Wallowing unweildie, enormous in thir Gate
Tempest the Ocean:

6c————

The crows and choughs that wing the midway air
Show scarce so gross as beetles: half way down
Hangs one that gathers samphire, dreadful trade!
Methinks he seems no bigger than his head:
The fishermen that walk upon the beach
Appear like mice; and yond tall anchoring bark
Diminished to her cock; her cock a buoy
Almost too small for sight: the murmuring surge
That on the unnumber'd idle pebbles chafes
Cannot be heard so high.

6d

between green
                mountains
sings the flinger
of

fire   beyond red rivers
of fair perpetual
feet the
sinuous

        riot

7a_____

Come Muse migrate from Greece and Ionia,
Cross out please those immensely overpaid accounts,
That matter of Troy and Achilles' wrath, and Aeneas',
    Odysseus' wanderings,
Placard "Removed" and "To Let" on the rocks of your snowy
    Parnassus,
Repeat at Jerusalem, place the notice high on Jaffa's gate and
    on Mount Moriah.
The same on the walls of your German, French, and Spanish
    castles, and Italian collections,
For know a better, fresher, busier sphere, a wide, untried
    domain awaits, demands you.

7b_____

Tell me, Muse, of that man who got around
After sacred Troy fell,
He knew men and cities,
His heart riled in the sea
As he strove for himself and his friends:
He did not save them.   Fools
They ate Hyperion's cattle
And He, the Sun, saw they never came home.
Tell us about it, my Light!
Start where you please!

8a_____

Madamé, ye ben of al beauté shryne,
As fer as cercléd is the mappémounde;
For as the cristal glorious ye shyne,
And lyké ruby ben your chekés rounde.
Therewith ye ben so mery and so jocounde,
That at a revel whan that I see you daunce,
It is an oynément unto my wounde,
Thogh ye to me ne do no daliaunce.

8b_____

Nay but you, who do not love her,
    Is she not pure gold, my mistress?
Holds earth aught — speak truth — above her?
    Aught like this tress, see, and this tress,
And this last fairest tress of all
So fair, see, ere I let it fall?

Because, you spend your lives in praising;
    To praise, you search the wide world over:
Then why not witness, calmly gazing,
    If earth holds aught — speak truth — above her?
Above this tress, and this, I touch
But cannot praise, I love so much!

9a_____

Hyd, Absolon, thy gilte tresses clere;
Ester, ley thou thy meknesse al a-doun;
Hyd, Jonathas, al thy frendly manere;
Penalopee, and Marcia Catoun,
Mak of your wyfhod no comparisoun;
Hyde ye your beautes, Isoude and Eleyne;
My lady cometh, that al this may disteyne. [1]

Thy faire body, lat hit [2] nat appere,
Lavyne; and thou, Lucresse of Rome toun,
And Polixene, that boghten love so dere,
And Cleopatre, with al thy passioun,
Hyde ye your trouthe of love and your renoun;
And thou, Tisbe, that hast of love swich peyne;
My lady cometh, that al this may disteyne.

Herro, Dido, Laudomia, alle y-fere, [3]
And Phyllis, hanging for thy Demophoun,
And Canace, espyed by thy chere,
Ysiphile, betraysed with Jasoun,
Maketh of your trouthe neyther boost ne soun;
Nor Ypermistere or Adriane, ye tweyne;
My lady cometh, that al this may disteyne.

(1) bedim; discolor   (2) it   (3) together

9b_____

Were [1] beth they biforen us weren,
Houndés ladden and haukés [2] beren,
   And hadden feld and wode,
      The riché levedies [3] in hoere [4] bour, [5]
      That wereden gold in hoere tressour,
   With hoere brightté rode? [6]

Eten and drounken and maden hem [7] glad;
Hoere lif was al with gamen ilad;
   Men keneleden [8] hem biforen

They beren hem wel swithé (9) heye
And in a twincling of an eye
Hoere soulés weren forloren. (10)

Were is that lawing (11) and that song,
That trayling and that proudé yong,
 Tho (12) hauekes and tho houndes?
 Al that joye is went away
 That wele (13) is comen to welaway
To many hardé stoundes. (14)

(1) where   (2) hawks   (3) ladies   (4) their   (5)bower
(6) complexion   (7) them   (8) kneeled   (9) very   (10) lost
(11) laughing   (12) those   (13) weal, fortune   (14) hours, times

9c

Hwer (1) is Paris and Heleyne,
 That weren so bryht and feyre on bleo? (2)
Amadas, Tristram and Dideyne,
 Yseude (3) and allé theo, (4)
Ector (5) with his scharpé meyne, (6)
 And Cesar rich of worldés feo? (7)
Heo (8) beoth (9) iglyden (10) ut (11) of the reyne, (12)
 So (13) the scheft (14) is of (15) the cleo. (16)

(1) where   (2) literally, dark blue; hue; "on bleo" equals perhaps in bleak
weather, in bleak times   (3) Isolde   (4) of them, those   (5) Hector
(6) mien; power   (7) goods; property; wealth   (8) they   (9) have
(10) glided   (11) out   (12) reins, "ut of the reyne" equals out of the
running   (13) as   (14) form; sheaf   (15) out of   (16) clay; steep
hillside

9d

Tell me now in what hidden way is
 Lady Flora the lovely Roman?
Where's Hipparchia, and where is Thais
 Neither of them the fairer woman?
 Where is Echo, beheld of no man,
Only heard on river and mere, —
 She whose beauty was more than human? . . .
But where are the snows of yester-year?

10a———

Like to these unmeasurable montaynes
    Is my painfull life the burden of Ire,
    For of great height be they, and high is my desire
And I of tears, and they be full of fountaynes;
Under craggy rockes they have full barren playns:
    Hard thoughtes in me, my wofull mind doth tire;
    Small fruit and many leaves their tops do attire:
Small effect with great trust in me remayns.
The boyseus winds oft their high boughs do blast:
    Hot sighs from me continually be shed;
    Cattle in them: and in me love is fed;
Immoveable am I: and they are full stedfast;
Of that restless birds they have the tune and note:
    And I always plaintes that passe through my throte.

10b———

What is your substance, whereof are you made,
That millions of strange shadows on you tend:
Since every one hath, every one, one shade,
And you, but one, can every shadow lend.
Describe Adonis, and the counterfeit
Is poorly imitated after you;
On Helen's cheek all art of beauty set,
And you in Grecian tires are painted new:
Speak of the spring and foison of the year,
The one doth shadow of your beauty show,
The other as your bounty doth appear;
And you in every blessèd shape we know.
    In all external grace you have some part,
    But you like none, none you, for constant heart.

11a_____

There was never nothing more me pained
    Nor nothing more me moved
As when my sweetheart her complained
    That ever she me loved.
                Alas the while!

With piteous look she said, and sighed:
    "Alas what aileth me,
"To love and set my wealth so light
    "On him that loveth not me."
                Alas the while!

"Was I not well void of all pain
    "When that nothing me grieved?
"And now with sorrows I must complain,
    "And cannot be relieved."
                Alas the while!

"My restful nights and joyful days
    "Since I began to love
"Be take from me, all thing decays
    "Yet can I not remove."
                Alas the while!

She wept and wrung her hands withal;
    The tears fell in my neck;
She turned her face and let it fall,
    Scarcely therewith could speak.
                Alas the while!

Her pains tormented me so sore
    That comfort had I none;
But cursed my fortune more and more
    To see her sob and groan;
                Alas the while!

11b_____

This other day
I heard a may
Right piteously complain.
She said alway
Without denay,
Her heart was full of pain.

She said, alas!
Without trespass,
Her dear heart was untrue.
'In every place
I wot he has
Forsake me for a new.'

'Adieu, farewell,
Adieu, *le bel*
Adieu, both friend and foe!
I cannot tell
Where I shall dwell;
My heart it grieveth me so.'

She had not said,
But at a braid [1]
Her dear heart was full near;
And said, 'Good maid,
Be not dismayed,
My love, my darling dear!'

In arms he hent [2]
That lady gent. [3]
In voiding care and moan,
That day they spent
To their intent
In wilderness alone.

[1] instant   [2] seized   [3] gentle

12a_____

Farewell, thou child of my right hand, and joy;
My sin was too much hope of thee, loved boy.
Seven years thou were lent to me, and I thee pay,
Exacted by thy fate, on the just day.
Oh, could I lose all father now! for why
Will man lament the state he should envy?
To have so soon 'scaped world's and flesh's rage,
And, if no other misery, yet age!
Rest in soft peace; and, asked, say, "Here doth lie
Ben Johnson his best piece of poetry,
For whose sake henceforth all his vows be such
As what he loves may never like too much."

12b_____

This rosemary is withered; pray, get fresh.
I would have these herbs grow up in his grave,
When I am dead and rotten. Reach the bays,
I'll tie a garland here about his head;
'Twill keep my boy from lightning. This sheet
I have kept this twenty year, and every day
Hallowed it with my prayers: I did not think
He should have wore it.

13a_____

> *Green groweth the holly; so doth the ivy.*
> *Though winter blastès blow never so high,*
> *Green groweth the holly.*

As the holly groweth green,
    And never changeth hue
So I am, ever hath been
    Unto my lady true;

As the holly groweth green,
    With ivy all alone,
When flowerès can not be seen
    And green wood leaves be gone.

Now unto my lady
    Promise to her I make,
From all other only
    To her I me betake.

Adieu, mine own lady,
    Adieu, my special,
Who hath my heart truly
    Be sure, and ever shall!

13b_____

Whoe'er she be —
That not impossible She
That shall command my heart and me:
       . . .
I wish her store
Of worth may leave her poor
Of wishes; and I wish — no more.

Now, if Time knows
That Her, whose radiant brows
Weave them a garland of my vows;

Her whose just bays
My future hopes can raise,
A trophy to her present praise;

Her that dares be
What these lines wish to see;
I seek no further, it is She.

14a_____

As virtuous men pass mildly away,
    And whisper to their soules, to go,
Whilst some of their sad friends do say,
    The breath goes now, and some say, no:

So let us melt, and make no noise,
    No tear-floods, nor sigh-tempests move,
T'were prophanation of our joys
    To tell the laity our love.

Moving of th' earth brings harms and fears,
    Men reckon what it did and meant,
But trepidation of the spheres,
    Though greater far, is innocent.

Dull sublunary lovers love
    (Whose soul is sense) cannot admit
Absence, because it doth remove
    Those things which elemented it.

But we by a love, so much refin'd
    That our selves know not what it is,
Inter-assured of the mind,
    Care less, eyes, lips and hands to miss.

Our two souls therefore, which are one,
    Though I must go, endure not yet
A breach, but an expansion,
    Like gold to airy thinness beat.

If they be two, they are two so
    As stiff twin compasses are two,
Thy soul the fixt foot, makes no show
    To move, but doth, if the'other do.

And though it in the center fit,
    Yet when the other far doth roam,
It leans, and hearkens after it,
    And grows erect, as that comes home.

Such wilt thou be to me, who must
    Like th' other foot, obliquely run;
Thy firmness makes my circle just,
    And makes me end, where I begun.

14b_____

My love is of a birth as rare
    As 'tis for object strange and high:
It was begotten of Despair
        Upon Impossibility.

Magnanimous Despair alone
    Could show me so divine a thing,
When feeble Hope could ne'er have flown,
        But vainly flapped its tinsel wing.

And yet I quickly might arrive
    Where my extended soul is fixt;
But Fate does iron wedges drive
        And always crowds itself betwixt.

For Fate with jealous eye does see
    Two perfect loves, nor lets them close;
Their union would her ruin be,
        And her tyrannic power depose.

And therefore her decrees of steel
    Us as distant poles have placed,
(Though Love's whole world on us doth wheel)
        Not by themselves to be embraced.

Unless the giddy heaven fall,
    And earth some new convulsion tear,
And, us to join, the world should all
        Be cramped into a planisphere.

As lines, so loves oblique, may well
    Themselves in every angle greet:

But ours, so truly parallel
      Though infinite, can never meet.

Therefore the love which us doth bind
    But Fate so enviously debars,
Is the conjunction of the mind,
      And opposition of the stars.

15a_____

So hath your beautè fro your herte [1] chaced
Pitee, that me ne availeth not to pleyne; [2]
For Daunger halt [3] your mercy in his cheyne. [4]

Giltles [5] my deeth thus han ye me purchaced;
I sey yow sooth, me needeth not to feyne; [6]
 So hath your beautè fro your herte chaced
 Pitee, that me ne availeth not to pleyne.

Allas! that nature hath in yow compassed
So greet beautè, that no man may atteyne
To mercy, though he sterve for the peyne.
 So hath your beautè fro your herte chaced
 Pitee, that me ne availeth not to pleyne;
 For Daunger halt your mercy in his cheyne.

(1) heart (2) complain (3) holds (4) chain (5) guiltless
(6) feign

15b_____

Now on the sea from her olde love comes she
That draws the day from heaven's cold axletree
Aurora wither slidest thou down againe
And brydes from Memnon yearly shall be slaine.
Now in her tender arms I sweetly bide,
If ever, now well lies she by my side,
The aire is cold and sleep is sweetest now
And birdes send forth shrill notes from every bough:
Wither runst thou, that men and women love not?
Hold in thy rosie horses that they move not!
Ere thou rise, stars teach seamen where to saile
But when thou comest, they of their courses faile.

16a_____

Follow thy fair sun, unhappy shadow;
    Though thou be black as night,
    And she made all of light,
Yet follow thy fair sun, unhappy shadow.

Follow her whose light thy light depriveth;
    Though here thou livest disgraced,
    And she in heaven is placed,
Yet follow her whose light the world reviveth.

Follow those pure beams whose beauty burneth,
    That so have scorchèd thee
    As thou still black must be
Till her kind beams thy black to brightness turneth.

Follow her, while yet her glory shineth:
    There comes a luckless night,
    That will dim all her light;
And this the black unhappy shade divineth.

Follow still, since so thy fates ordainèd:
    The sun must have his shade,
    Till both at once do fade;
The sun still proved, the shadow still disdainèd.

16b_____

Do not conceal thy radiant eyes,
The star-light of serenest skies,
Lest wanting of their heavenly light,
They turn to Chaos' endless night.

Do not conceal those tresses fair,
The silken snares of thy curl'd hair,
Lest finding neither gold, nor ore,
The curious silkworm work no more.

131

Do not conceal those breasts of thine,
More snow-white than the Apennine,
Lest if there be like cold or frost,
The lily be for ever lost.

Do not conceal that fragrant scent,
Thy breath, which to all flowers hath lent
Perfumes, lest it being supprest,
No spices grow in all the East.

Do not conceal thy heavenly voice,
Which makes the hearts of gods rejoice,
Lest Music hearing no such thing,
The Nightingale forget to sing.

Do not conceal, nor yet eclipse
Thy pearly teeth with coral lips,
Lest that the seas cease to bring forth
Gems, which from thee have all their worth.

Do not conceal no beauty grace,
That's either in thy mind or face,
Lest virtue overcome by vice
Make men believe no Paradise.

17a———

God be with trewthé where he be!
I wolde he were in this cuntre.

A man that schuld of trewthé [1] telle
With grete lordès he may not dwelle.
In trewé story as clerkès telle
    Trewthé is put in low degree.

In laydies chaumberes cometh he not;
There dare trewthé setten none [2] fot. [2]
Thow he woldé, he may not
    Comen among the heye mené. [3]

With men of lawe he hath non spas; [4]
They loven trewthe in none plas
Me thinketh they han a rewly [5] grace
    That trewthe is put at swich degree.

In holy cherche he may not sitte;
Fro man to man they schuln him flitte.
It reweth me sore in mine witte,
    Of trewthe I have gret pité.

Religious, that schulde be good,
If trewthe cum there, I holde him wood. [6]
They schulden [7] him rende cote and hood,
    And make him bare for to flee.

A man that schulde of trewthe aspie
He must seken esilye
In the bosum of Marie
    For there he is for sothe.

(1) truth   (2) no foot   (3) meinie, company   (4) space   (5) pitiable
(6) mad   (7) would

17b———

He knew the seat of Paradise,
Could tell in what degree it lies

And, as he was disposed, could prove it
Below the moon or else above it:
What Adam dreamt of when his bride
Came from her closet in his side,
Whether the devil tempted her
By an High-Dutch interpreter,
If either of them had a navel,
Who first made music malleable
Whether the serpent at the fall
Had cloven feet or none at all,
All this without a gloss or comment
He could unriddle in a moment
In proper terms such as men smatter
When they throw out and miss the matter.

. . .

Whate'er men speak by this new light,
Still they are sure to be i' th' right,
'Tis a dark lanthorn of the spirit
Which none see by but those who bear it.

. . .

A light that falls down from on high
For spiritual trades to cozen by,
An ignis fatuus that bewitches
And leads men into pools and ditches
To make dip themselves and sound
For Christendom in dirty pond,
To dive like wild fowl for salvation
And fish to catch regeneration.

18a_____

Farewell to these; but all our poor to know,
Let's seek the winding lane, the narrow row —
Suburbian prospects, where the traveller stops
To see the sloping tenement on props,
With building yards immix'd, and humble sheds and shops;
Where the Cross-Keys and Plumber's-Arms invite
Laborious men to taste their coarse delight;
Where the low porches, stretching from the door,
Gave some distinction in the days of yore —
Yet now, neglectèd, more offend the eye
By gloom and ruin than the cottage by.
Places like these the noblest town endures,
The gayest place has its sinks and sewers.

Here is no pavement, no inviting shop,
To give us shelter when compell'd to stop;
But plashy puddles stand along the way
Fill'd by the rain of one tempestuous day;
And these so closely to the buildings run,
That you must ford them, for you cannot shun;
Though here and there convenient bricks are laid,
And door-side heaps afford their dubious aid . . .
There, fed by food they love, to rankest size
Around the dwelling docks and wormwood rise; . . .
Then will I lead thee down the dusty row,
By the warm alley and the long close lane —
There mark the fractured door and paper'd pane,
Where flags the noon-tide air, and, as we pass,
We fear to breathe the putrefying mass.
But fearless yonder matron; she disdains
To sigh for zephyrs from ambrosial plains;
But mends her meshes torn, and pours her lay
All in the stifling fervour of the day.

Her naked children round the alley run,
And, roll'd in dust, are bronzed beneath the sun;

Or gambol round the dame, who, loosely dress'd,
Woos the coy breeze, to fan the open breast.

18b_____

Barefoot and ragged, with neglected hair,
She whom the Heavens at once made poor and fair,
    With humble voice and moving words did stay,
    To beg an alms of all who pass'd that way.

But thousands viewing her became her prize,
Willingly yielding to her conquering eyes,
    And caught by her bright hairs, whilst careless she
    Makes them pay homage to her poverty.

So mean a boon, said I, what can extort
From that fair mouth, where wanton Love to sport
    Amidst the pearl and rubies we behold?
Nature on thee has all her treasures spread,
Do but incline thy rich and precious head,
    And those fair locks shall pour down showers of gold.

19a_____

Welcom be ye whan ye go,
    And farewell whan ye come;
So faire as ye there be no mo
    As bright as bery broune.
I love you verrily at my to,
    Nonne so moche in all this toune;
I am right glad when ye will go,
    And sory when ye will come.

And whan ye be other fare
    I pray for you sertaine,
That never manner horsse ne mare
    Bringe you to towne agein.
To praise your beauté I ne dare,
    For drede that men wille seyn;
Farewelle, no more for you I care,
    But pray you of my songe have no desdein.

19b_____

O saw ye bonnie Lesley
    As she gaed o'er the border?
She's gane, like Alexander,
    To spread her conquests farther.

To see her is to love her,
    And love but her for ever;
For Nature made her what she is,
    And never made anither!

Thou art a queen, fair Lesley,
    Thy subjects we, before thee:
Thou art divine, fair Lesley,
    The hearts o' men adore thee.

The Deil he could na scaith thee,
    Or aught that wad belang thee;

He'd look into thy bonnie face,
    And say, 'I canna wrang thee.'

The Powers aboon will tent thee;
    Misfortune sha' na steer thee;
Thou'rt like themselves sae lovely,
    That ill they'll ne'er let near thee.

Return again, fair Lesley,
    Return to Caledonie!
That we may brag we hae a lass
    There's nane again sae bonnie.

20a

Poor naked wretches, wheresoe'er you are,
That bide the pelting of this pitiless storm,
How shall your houseless heads and unfed sides,
Your loop'd and window'd raggedness, defend you
From seasons such as these? O, I have ta'en
Too little care of this! Take physic, pomp;
Expose thyself to feel what wretches feel,
That thou mayst shake the superflux to them
And show the heavens more just.

20b

And the creature run from the cur? There
thou mightst behold the great image of authority: a
dog's obeyed in office.
Thou rascal beadle, hold thy bloody hand!
Why dost thou lash that whore? Strip thine own back;
Thou hotly lust'st to use her in that kind
For which thou whip'st her. The usurer hangs the cozener.
Through tattered clothes small vices do appear;
Robes and furr'd gowns hide all. Plate sin with gold,
And the strong lance of justice hurtless breaks;
Arm it in rags, a pigmy's straw does pierce it.
None does offend, none, I say, none; I'll able 'em:
Take that of me, my friend, who have the power
To seal the accuser's lips. Get thee glass eyes,
And, like a scurvy politician, seem
To see the things thou dost not.
Now, now, now, now: pull off my boots: harder,
    harder: so.

20c

Pour the unhappiness out
From your too bitter heart
Which grieving will not sweeten.

Poison grows in this dark.
It is in the water of tears
Its black blooms rise.

The magnificient cause of being —
The imagination, the one reality
In this imagined world —

Leaves you
With him for whom no fantasy moves,
And you are pierced by a death.

21a———

Give yourself no unnecessary pain,
My dear Lord Cardinal. Here, Mother, tie
My girdle for me, and bind up this hair
In any simple knot; aye, that does well.
And yours I see is coming down. How often
Have we done this for one another; now
We shall not do it any more. My Lord,
We are quite ready. Well, 'tis very well.

21b———

For thee, my own sweet sister, in thy heart
I know myself secure, as thou in mine;
We were and are — I am, even as thou art —
Beings who ne'er each other can resign;
It is the same, together or apart,
From life's commencement to its slow decline
We are entwined — let death come slow or fast
The tie which bound the first endures the last.

21c———

Shall we not see these daughters and these sisters?
No, no, no, no! Come, let's away to prison:
We two alone will sing like birds i' the cage:
When thou dost ask me blessing, I'll kneel down
And ask of thee forgiveness: so we'll live
And pray, and sing, and tell old tales, and laugh
At gilded butterflies, and hear poor rogues
Talk of court news; and we'll talk with them too,
Who loses and who wins, who's in, who's out;

And take upon's the mystery of things,
As if we were God's spies: and we'll wear out,
In a wall'd prison, packs and sects of great ones
That ebb and flow by the moon.
                              Wipe thine eyes;
The good-years shall devour them, flesh and fell,
Ere they shall make us weep: we'll see 'em starve first.
Come.

22a_____

To the dim light and the large circle of shade
I have clomb, and to the whitening of the hills,
There where we see no colour in the grass.
Nathless my longing loses not its green,
It has so taken root in the hard stone
Which talks and hears as though it were a lady.

Utterly frozen is this youthful lady
Even as the snow that lies within the shade;
For she is no more moved than is the stone
By the sweet season which makes warm the hills
And alters them afresh from white to green,
Covering their sides again with flowers and grass.

When on her hair she sets a crown of grass
The thought has no more room for other lady,
Because she weaves the yellow with the green
So well that Love sits down there in the shade, —
Love who has shut me in among low hills
Faster than between walls of granite-stone.

She is more bright than is a precious stone;
The wound she gives may not be healed with grass:
I therefore have fled far o'er plains and hills
For refuge from so dangerous a lady;
But from her sunshine nothing can give shade, —
Not any hill, nor wall, nor summer-green.

A while ago, I saw her dressed in green, —
So fair, she might have wakened in a stone
This love which I do feel even for her shade,
And therefore, as one woos a graceful lady,
I wooed her in a field that was all grass
Girdled about with very lofty hills.

Yet shall the streams turn back and climb the hills
Before Love's flame in this damp wood and green
Burn, as it burns within a youthful lady,

For my sake, who would sleep away in stone
My life, or feed like beasts upon the grass,
Only to see her garments cast a shade.

How dark soe'er the hills throw out their shade,
Under her summer-green the beautiful lady
Covers it, like a stone covered in grass.

22b_____

With other women I beheld my love; —
    Not that the rest were women to mine eyes,
Who only as her shadows seemed to move.

I do not praise her more than with the truth,
    Nor blame I these if it be rightly read.
But while I speak, a thought I may not soothe
    Says to my senses: "Soon shall ye be dead,
      If for my sake your tears ye will not shed."

And then the eyes yield passage, at that thought,
To the heart's weeping, which forgets her not.

22c_____

I

Like the sweet apple which reddens upon the topmost bough
A-top on the topmost twig, — which the pluckers forgot
    somehow, —
Forgot it not, nay, but got it not, for none could get it
    till now.

II

Like the wild hyacinth flower which on the hills is found,
Which the passing feet of the shepherds for ever tear
    and wound,
Until the purple blossom is trodden into the ground.

22d

I will write songs against you,
enemies of my people; I will pelt you
with the winged seeds of the dandelion;
I will marshal against you
the fireflies of the dusk.

22e———

How shall we mourn you who are killed and wasted,
Sure that you would not die with your work unended,
As if the iron scythe in the grass stops for a flower?

23a_____

Look for the nul
defeats it all

the N of all
equations

that rock, the blank
that holds them up

which pulled away —
the rock's

their fall. Look
for that nul

that's past all
seeing

the death of all
that's past

all being

23b_____

Love, love, nothing but love, still more!
    For, O, love's bow
    Shoots buck and doe.
    The shaft confounds,
    Not that it wounds,
But tickles still the sore.
These lovers cry Oh! ho! they die!
    Yet that which seems the wound to kill,
Doth turn oh! ho! to ha! ha! he!
    So, dying, love lives still.
Oh! ho! a while, but ha! ha! ha!
Oh! ho! groans out for ha! ha! ha!

23c_____

That day of wrath, that dreadful day,
When heaven and earth shall pass away,
What power shall be the sinner's stay?
How shall he meet that dreadful day?

23d_____

cried the third crumb, i am should
and this is my little sister could
with our big brother who is would
don't punish us for we were good;

and the last crumb with some shame
whispered unto God, my name
is must and with the others i've
been Effie who isn't alive

24a_____

Your thighs are appletrees
whose blossoms touch the sky.
Which sky? The sky
where Watteau hung a lady's
slipper. Your knees
are a southern breeze — or
a gust of snow. Agh! what
sort of man was Fragonard?
— as if that answered
anything. Ah, yes — below
the knees, since the tune
drops that way, it is
one of those white summer days,
the tall grass of your ankles
flickers upon the shore —
Which shore?
the sand clings to my lips —
Which shore?
Agh, petals maybe. How
should I know?
Which shore? Which shore?
I said petals from an appletree.

24b_____

Sitting alone (as one forsook)
Close by a Silver-shedding Brook;
With hands held up to Love, I wept;
And after sorrowes spent, I slept:
Then in a Vision I did see
A glorious forme appeare to me:
A Virgins face she had; her dresse
Was like a sprightly Spartanesse.
A silver bow with green silk strung
Down from her comely shoulders hung:

And as she stood, the wanton Aire
Dangled the ringlets of her haire.
Her legs were such Diana shows,
When tuckt up she a-hunting goes;
With Buskins shortned to descrie
The happy dawning of her thigh:
Which when I saw, I made accesse
To kisse that tempting nakednesse:
But she forbad me, with a wand
Of Mirtle she had in her hand:
And chiding me, said, Hence, Remove,
Herrick, thou art too coorse to love.

25a_____

Forty-leben days gone by
Sence last time ah slept in bed
Ah ain' had three squares sence ah was bawn
Money thinks ahm dead
Money thinks ahm dead

Chain gang link is waitin'
Ah ain' done nothin' 'tall
A place to sleep, somethin' to eat
Ah don' ast fo' chain an' ball
Ah don' ast fo' chain an' ball

Clothes am torn to pieces
Shoes am all worn out
Ahm rollin' through an unfrien'ly Worl'
Always wanderin' 'bout
Lawd always wanderin' 'bout

25b_____

I tried to put a bird in a cage.
  O fool that I am!
 For the bird was Truth.
Sing merrily, Truth: I tried to put
  Truth in a cage!

And when I had the bird in the cage,
  O fool that I am!
 Why, it broke my pretty cage.
Sing merrily, Truth; I tried to put
  Truth in a cage!

And when the bird was flown from the cage,
  O fool that I am!
 Why, I had nor bird nor cage.
Sing merrily, Truth! I tried to put
  Truth in a cage!
  Heigh-ho! Truth in a cage.

25c_____

Poetry

I too, dislike it; there are things
  that are important beyond all this fiddle. Reading it,
    however, with a perfect contempt for it,
      one discovers that there is in it, after all, a place for the
        genuine:
        hands that can grasp, eyes that can dilate, hair that
        can rise if it must,

the bat holding on upside down,
  an elephant pushing, a tireless wolf under a tree,
    the immovable critic twitching his skin
      like a horse that feels a fly, the base-ball fan, the statis-
        tician — nor is it
        valid to discriminate against business documents,
        school-books,

trade reports — these phenomena
  are important; but dragged into conscious oddity by
    half poets, the result is not poetry.
      This we know. In a liking for the raw material in all
        its rawness,
        and for that which is genuine, there is liking for poetry.

CHRONOLOGICAL CHART

PART I

1. Homer, *Odyssey* XI
   translated by
   a. George Chapman ... 1616
   b. Thomas Hobbes ... 1673
   c. Adaptation ... 1948

2. Homer, *Odyssey* XI
   a. Adaptation ... 1948
   b. Alexander Pope ... 1725
   c. W. C. Bryant ... 1871

3. Ovid, *Metamorphoses* I
   translated by
   a. John Dryden
      Third Miscellany ... 1693
   b. Arthur Golding ... 1565

4. Ovid, *Metamorphoses*
   translated by
   Arthur Golding ... 1565
   a. Bk. I
   b. Bk. III

5. a. Catullus, *CXV*
      translated by
      F. W. Cornish ... 1913
   b. Thomas Hood
      *Miss Kilmansegg and
      Her Precious Leg* ... 1840

PART II

1. a. Homer, *Iliad* III
      translated by
      Alexander Pope ... 1715
   b. Wm. Shakespeare
      *Troilus and
      Cressida*, II, ii ... 1602

2. Homer, *Odyssey* XI
   translated by
   a. Thomas Hobbes ... c. 1673-7
   b. William Morris ... 1897

3. a. Ovid, *Elegies* III, 8
      translated by
      Christopher Marlowe ... c. 1590
   b. Samuel Johnson ... 1749
      The Vanity of Human Wishes

4. a. Wm. Shakespeare
      Venus and Adonis ... 1593
   b. Ovid, *Metamorphoses*
      Bk. VIII
      translated by
      Arthur Golding ... 1565

5. Catullus, *Ad Lesbiam*
   translated by
   a. Lord Byron ... 1807
   b. Sir Philip Sidney ... c. 1579

* To be consulted casually *after* reading all 3 parts.
** To the author, in casual retrospect, the critical matter of Part II may be summed up under the heads listed; anyone else must sum it up as it appears to him.

CHART *

CONSIDERATION**	PART III

Translation

1. a. Homer, *Odyssey* **XI**
      translated by
      George Chapman   1616
   b. Mark Van Doren
      Death   1928
   c. Sadi, *Gulistan* I, 4   1258
      translated by
      Basil Bunting   c. 1935
   d. *I. Samuel*, 28
      King James Version   1611

Speech

2. Lucretius *De Rerum Natura* I
   translated by
   a. John Dryden
      Second Miscellany   1685
   b. Basil Bunting
      To Venus, after Lucretius
         1930

Definition

3. Ovid, *Elegies* I, 15
   translated by
   a. Christopher Marlowe   1586
   b. Ben Jonson
      The Poetaster I, i   1601-2

Sight

4. a. Ovid, *Metamorphoses*
      translated by
      Arthur Golding   1565
   b. Wm. Shakespeare
      The Tempest, V, i   1611

Measure

5. a. Catullus, CI
      translated by
      F. W. Cornish   1913
   b. Walt Whitman
      When Lilacs Last   1865
   c. E. E. Cummings
      Is 5   1926

PART I	PART II

6. **a.** Virgil, *The Aeneid*
    translated by
    Gawin Douglas   1512-13
    b. Wm. Shakespeare
    The Tempest, I, ii   1611

6. a. Virgil, *The Aeneid*
    translated by
    Gawin Douglas   1512-13
    b. Wm. Shakespeare
    Pericles, III, i   1609

7. a. Robert Herrick
    *To Live Merrily and to
    Trust to Good Verses*   1648
    b. Ovid, *Elegies* I, 15
    translated by
    Christopher Marlowe   1586

7. Ovid, *Elegies*
    translated by
    Christopher Marlowe   c. 1590
    a. Bk. I, 1
    b. Bk. III, 1

8. a. *A Lyke-Wake Dirge*   15c.
    b. *Carol*   15c.
    c. from collection by
    Robert Thornton of
    East Newton, Yorkshire
    c. 1440
    (attributed to
    Richard Rolle of Hampole)

8. *Alisoun*
    a. Southern English dialect
    original   late 13c. — early 14c.
    b. translated by
    J. L. Weston   1913

9. a. Francois Villon   1450
    *Epistle in Form of a
    Ballade to his Friends*
    translated by
    A. C. Swinburne   1878
    b. Geoffrey Chaucer
    *Balade, Lak of
    Stedfastnesse*   c. 1380-96

9. a. Geoffrey Chaucer
    The Book of the Duchesse
    1369
    b. Francois Villon   1450
    Rondeau, translated by
    D. G. Rossetti   c. 1870
    c. Anonymous
    O western wind   16c.

157

PART I	PART II

10. Thomas Wyatt   1503-42
   a. *They fle from me*
   b. *The long love*
     (in Tottel's
     Songes and Sonettes)   1557

10. a. Mark Alexander Boyd
                1563-1601
     Sonet
   b. Edmund Spenser
     The Visions of
     Petrarch   1590

11. a. Anonymous Ballad   15c.
     Robin Hood Rescuing Three
     Squires, from F. J. Child's
     Coll. Ballads, Vol. III
                1888-90
   b. Same as 11a.

11. a. Anonymous
     Walsinghame   16c.
   b. Anonymous
     Robin Hood Ballad   16c.

12. Wm. Shakespeare
   a. *A Midsummer-Night's*
     Dream, III, ii   1600
   b. Same as 12a.
   c. *King Lear*, IV, i   1607

12. a. Wm. Shakespeare
     King Lear, IV, i   1608
   b. John Milton
     Samson Agonistes   1667-71

13. a. Wm. Shakespeare
     The Phoenix and Turtle
                1601
   b. John Milton
     Samson Agonistes   1667-71

13. a. Wm. Shakespeare
     Hamlet, IV, v   1603
   b. John Webster
     The Duchess of Malfi,
     IV, ii   1616

14. John Donne   1573-1631
   a. *The Extasie*, first
     published   1633
   b. Same as 14a.

14. Wm. Shakespeare
   a. *Sonnet* 116   1608-9
   b. *A Midsummer-Night's*
     Dream, I, i   1594-5

CONSIDERATION	PART III

159

PART I	PART II

15. a. Anonymous 17c.
    b. John Donne
       The Dream, first
       published 1633
    c. John Fletcher
       from *The Beggar's Bush* 1647

15. a. George Herbert 1593-1632
       The Collar
    b. Thomas Fuller
       The Holy State 1641

16. a. Robert Herrick
       To Daffadils 1648
    b. Robert Herrick
       *Divination by a
       Daffadil* 1648
    c. Louis Zukofsky
       Little Wrists 1948

16. Robert Herrick
    a. *Violets* c. 1648
    b. *To Keep a True Lent* 1648

17. a. Lord Rochester
       (John Wilmot)
       Ode to Nothing c. 1670
    b. Edward Fitzgerald
       *Rubaiyat of Omar
       Khayyam* 1859
    c. William Butler Yeats
       Blood and the Moon II 1928

17. a. Alexander Pope
       Dunciad 1728
    b. George Crabbe
       Inebriety, I 1775
    c. Earl of Rochester
       A Letter from Artemesia
       c. 1670
    d. Same as 17c.
    e. T. S. Eliot
       The Waste Land 1922

18. a. George Crabbe
       The Borough 1810
    b. Arthur Golding
       tr. Ovid,
       Metamorphoses, III 1565

18. a. George Crabbe
       The Borough, XXIII 1810
    b. Wm. Wordsworth
       Laodamia 1814

160

CONSIDERATION

PART I	PART II

<table>
<tr><td>

19. Robert Burns
  a. *Address to the Deil*   1786
  b. *Holy Willie's Prayer* c. 1790

</td><td>

19. Robert Burns
  a. *A Winter Night*   1786
  b. Same as 19a.
  c. *For A' That and A'*
    That   1794

</td></tr>
<tr><td>

20. a. Wm. Wordsworth
    Simon Lee   1800
  b. Waly, Waly   16 - 17c.
  c. Wm. Blake   1757-1827
    The Chimney Sweeper
  d. Lord Byron
    Oh! snatched away   1815

</td><td>

20. a. P. B. Shelley
    An Indian Serenade   1819
  b. Gerard Manley Hopkins
    Moonrise   1876

</td></tr>
<tr><td>

21. a. Robert Browning
    Sordello I   c. 1837
  b. Wm. C. Williams
    Paterson I   1946

</td><td>

21. a. Robert Browning   1868-9
    The Ring and the Book II
  b. Walter Savage Landor
    Epithalamium   c. 1831

</td></tr>
<tr><td>

22. a. Robert Browning
    Pippa Passes II   1841
  b. A. C. Swinburne
    Atalanta in Calydon   1865
  c. Robert Burns
    Lassie wi' the Lint-white
    Locks   1794
    (Tune of Rothiemurchie's
    Rant)
  d. George Peele
    Batshebe Sings
    (from *The Love of King*
    David and Bathsabe with the
    Tragedy of Absolom) 1599
  e. Robert Browning
    Pippa Passes III   1841

</td><td>

22. a. Robert Browning
    Pippa Passes   1841
  b. A. C. Swinburne
    Atalanta in Calydon   1865

</td></tr>
</table>

| | 19. | a. | Anonymous
South England | c. 1450 |
| Energy | | b. | Robert Burns
Bonnie Lesley | 1792 |

	20.	a.	Wm. Shakespeare *King Lear* III, iv	1607
Duration		b.	Wm. Shakespeare *King Lear* IV, v	
		c.	Wallace Stevens *Another Weeping* *Woman*	c. 1917
			(in *Harmonium*)	1923

	21.	a.	P. B. Shelley *The Cenci,* V	1819
Impact		b.	Lord Byron *Epistle to Augusta*	1816
		c.	Wm. Shakespeare *King Lear,* V, iii	1607

	22.	a.	Dante	1265-1321
			Canzone, I translated by D. G. Rossetti	c. 1861
		b.	Guido Cavalcanti	
				c. 1250-1300
			Ballata translated by D. G. Rossetti	1861
Movement		c.	D. G. Rossetti translator, *Beauty (A Combination* *from Sappho)*	c. 1861
		d.	Charles Reznikoff *Insignificance* I (in *Separate Way*)	1936
		e.	Charles Reznikoff XIV, *First Group* (in *Five Groups of Verse*)	
				1918

PART I

23. a. John Keats
    To Autumn 1820
    b. Lord Herbert
    of Cherbury 1581-1648
    *In a Glass Window for
    Inconstancy*
    c. Wm. Shakespeare
    Pericles, I, i 1609
    d. Lorine Niedecker c. 1935
    (in *New Goose*, 1946)

24. a. Thomas Wyatt
    Tagus, farewell 1539
    b. Wm. Shakespeare
    Pericles, I, ii 1609

25. a. H. C. Work
    The Year of Jubilee 1865
    b. Anonymous c. 1308-18
    Anglo-Irish Dialect
    c. Richard Edwards 1523-66
    Amantum Irae

PART II

23. a. John Skelton
    *To Mistress
    Margaret Hussey* 16c.
    b. Thomas Hardy
    Timing Her c. 1916

24. a. Anonymous
    I have a gentil cok 15c.
    b. Wm. C. Williams
    Spring and All 1923

25. a. H. C. Work
    The Year of Jubilee 1865
    b. Anonymous c. 1308-18
    Anglo-Irish Dialect

CONSIDERATION

165

ABOUT THE AUTHOR

Louis Zukofsky (1904–1978) was born on the Lower East Side of Manhattan. His early work, including his first published poem, "Poem Beginning 'The'," strived to establish the poem as object by employing syntactic fragmentation and line breaks that disrupt normal speech rhythm. Zukofsky invented the term "objectivist" and is widely considered one of the primary forerunners of contemporary avant-garde writing. His many books include *"A"*, *Prepositions*, *Bottom: on Shakespeare*, *The Complete Short Poetry*, and *The Collected Fiction*.

Library of Congress Cataloging-in-Publication Data

Zukofsky, Louis, 1904–1978.
    A test of poetry / Louis Zukofsky.
        p.   cm.—(the Wesleyan centennial edition of the complete critical writings
    of Louis Zukofsky ; v. 1)
    ISBN 0-8195-6402-8 (pa. : alk. paper)
        1. Poetry—Collections. I. Title.

PN6101.Z8   2000
808.81—dc21
                                                    99-48544